ISBN INFO

Dedicated to Claudia

Contents

Why Now, Why You, Why Me?

Americans need something new to believe in. It's not money, it's not owning a home, it's not a safe corporate job. The American religion is dead. We need to know that it's OK to fail. It's OK to be persistent. To have techniques that fire up our creativity, our energy, our health, our drive for success, ambition, and then ultimately meaning.

In the chapter, "How to Be the Luckiest Person Alive", I describe how you can unleash the core that will drive you from desire to ambition to meaning. In other chapters, I describe some of the paths I took along the way.

Why now?

The country is in post-traumatic stress syndrome. We got hit by 9/11 and the dot-com bust. We got hit by the corruptions of Enron, Worldcom, Madoff, and countless others. We got hit by the housing crisis, the fiscal crisis, the mass confusion emanating from government. What the hell are we doing in two wars ten years later? Maybe even three or four wars. Who is counting anymore? We got hit by 10% unemployment which underlined that no job is safe. All the jobs shipped off to China and are never coming back.

We can't sell our homes. We can't get jobs. Industries are vomiting up the last food they digested before they finally die (book stores, book publishers, video industry, the steel industry, record labels, even many computer companies, car companies, etc.)

But there's good news. The economy survived. The country survived. Look around you. You survived. You are alive. You are lucky.

Why you?

It's not about corporations anymore. It's not, "how do we market McDonalds so they can sell a few more hamburgers to our morbidly obese children?"

Now it's about how you heal yourself, make yourself a better person. Stay healthier: physically, emotionally, mentally, financially, and spiritually.

Becoming lucky is not about subscribing to a new religion. Nor is it about creating a new successful business. Its about becoming an entrepreneur in every aspect of your life. It's about finding your personal frontiers and exploring those edges. Exploration is dangerous. But leads to discovery and realization.

Its several steps:

Know that it's OK to have failed. We've all had nights where we look into the dark and say, "where the hell am I?"

Begin to use the luck you will learn here to take advantage of the opportunities that fall into your path.

Begin building a discipline from the core outwards where just by the rules of the universe, luck becomes attracted to you.

And with an extra several trillion dollars now that the economy has survived and the financial printing press is running, if you don't take advantage of those opportunities than someone else will.

Why Me?

Why not?

CHAPTER ONE
How to be the Luckiest Person Alive

I told my dad, "I'm a lucky guy." He said, "But are you lucky in love?" I was six years old. Love was the most disgusting thing in the world to me. What the hell was he talking about? Love was living in another neighborhood at that time. Or another planet. It would be years before Love stuck its ugly little nose into my house and said, "Hello, anyone here?

Luck was all about rolling the dice. Or finding a quarter on the ground. Or seeing a double rainbow after a quick storm.

But now I'm different. I'm constantly checking in and out of the Hospital of No Luck. I'm older. I need luck to be constantly transfused into me or I run out of it. Without luck, I'm dead. For me, good luck equals happiness. On a scale of happiness from 0 to 10, I think I'm about a nine.

But that's a big improvement. When I was lying on the floor after my divorce, or after my first big business failed, or after I lost my beautiful apartment in NYC, or after I lost my father, I was probably about a zero. Or at different points in this story, I was maybe at negative. So I'm trending upwards. I get lucky when I stick to three simple goals:

My ONLY Three Goals in Life

A)   I want to be happy.

B)   I want to eradicate unhappiness in my life.

C)   I want every day to be as smooth as possible. No hassles.

That's it. I'm not asking for much. I need simple goals else I can't achieve them.

There's been at least ten times in my life that everything seemed so low I felt like I would never achieve the above three things and the world would be better off without me. Other times I felt like I was stuck at a crossroads and would never figure out which road to take. Each time I bounced back.

When I look back at these times now I realize there was a common thread. Each time there were four things, and only four things, that were always in place in order for me to bounce back. Now I try to incorporate these four things into a daily practice so I never dip low again.

The Daily Practice

A)   **Physical** – being in shape. Doing some form of exercise. In 2003 I woke up at 5am every day and from 5-6am I played "Round the World" on a basketball court overlooking the Hudson River. Every day (except when it rained). Trains would pass and people at 5:30am would wave to me out the window. Now, I try to do yoga every day. But it's hard. All you need to do, minimally, is exercise enough to break a sweat for 10 minutes. So about 20-30 minutes worth of exercise a day. This is not to get "ripped" or "shredded". But just to be healthy. You can't be happy if you aren't healthy. Also, spending this time helps your mind better deal with its daily anxieties. If you can breathe easy when your body is in pain then it's easier to breathe during difficult situations. Here are other things that are a part of this but a little bit harder:

Wake up by 4-5am every day.

Go to sleep by 8:30-9. (Good to sleep 8 hours a night!)

No eating after 5:30pm. Can't be happy if indigested at night.

B)   **Emotional**– If someone is a drag on me I cut them out. If someone lifts me up, I bring them closer. Nobody is sacred here. When the plane is going down, put the oxygen mask on your face first. Family, friends, and people I love – I always try to be there for them and help. But I don't get close to anyone bringing me down. This rule can't be broken. Energy leaks out of you if someone is draining you. And I never owe anyone an explanation. Explaining is draining.

This doesn't mean abandon those who need you. Quite the opposite. If you are a clean river, then people can drink from you. If you are dirty water, then people will get sick.

Another important rule: always be honest. It's fun. Nobody is honest anymore and people are afraid of it. Try being honest for a day (without being hurtful). It's amazing where the boundaries are of how honest one can be. It's much bigger than I thought. A corollary of this is: I never do anything I don't want to do. Like I NEVER go to weddings.

C)   **Mental** – Every day I write down ideas. I write down so many ideas that it hurts my head to come up with one more. Then I try to write down five more. The other day I tried to write 100 alternatives kids can do other than go to college. I wrote down eight. I couldn't come up with anymore. Then the next day I came up with another 40. It definitely stretched my head. No ideas today? Memorize all the legal 2 letter words for Scrabble. Translate the Tao Te Ching into Spanish. Need ideas for lists of ideas? Come up with 30 separate chapters for an "autobiography". Try to think of 10 businesses you can start from home (and be realistic how you can execute them?). Think of 20 ways Obama can improve the country. List every productive thing you did yesterday (this improves memory also and gives you ideas for today).

The "idea muscle" atrophies within days if you don't use it. Just like walking. If you don't use your legs for a week, they atrophy. You need to exercise the idea muscle. It takes about 3-6 months to build up once it atrophies. Trust me on this.

You can get 100 waiter pads for almost nothing at any number of restaurant supply shops on the Internet. Use waiter pads. This forces you to list things rather than write. And you feel a sense of accomplishment by filling up pages quickly. Plus its cheap.

D)   **Spiritual**. I feel that most people don't like the word "spiritual". They think it means "god". Or "religion". But it doesn't. I don't know what it means actually. But I feel like I have a spiritual practice when I do one of the following:

Pray (doesn't matter if I'm praying to a god or to dead people or to the sun or to a chair in front of me – it just means being thankful. And not taking all the credit, for just a few seconds of the day).

Meditate – Meditation for more than a few minutes is hard. It's boring. You can also meditate for 15 seconds by really visualizing what it would be like meditate for 60 minutes. Here's a simple meditation: sit in a chair, keep the back straight, watch yourself breathe. If you get distracted, no problem. Just pull yourself back to your breath. Try it for 5 minutes. Then six.

Being grateful – I try to think of everyone in my life I'm grateful for. Then I try to think of more people. Then more. It's hard.

Forgiving – I picture everyone who has done me wrong. I visualize gratefulness for them (but not pity).

Studying. If I read a spiritual text (doesn't matter what it is: Bible, Tao Te Ching, anything Zen related, even inspirational self-help stuff, doesn't matter) I tend to feel good. This is not as powerful as praying or meditating (it doesn't train your mind to cut out the BS) but it still makes me feel good.

My own experience: I can never achieve the three "simple" goals on a steady basis without doing the above practice on a daily basis. And EVERY TIME I've hit bottom (or close to a bottom or I've been at some sort of crossroads.) and started doing the above 4 items (1991, 1995, 1997, 2002, 2006, 2008) magic would happen:

The Results

A)   Within about one month, I'd notice coincidences start to happen. I'd start to feel lucky. People would smile at me more.

B)   Within three months the ideas would really start flowing, to the point where I felt overwhelming urges to execute the ideas.

C)   Within six months, good ideas would start flowing, I'd begin executing them, and everyone around me would help me put everything together.

D)   Within a year my life was always completely different. 100% upside down from the year before. More money, more luck, more health, etc. And then I'd get lazy and stop doing the practice. And everything falls apart again. But now I'm trying to do it every day.

It's hard to do all of this every day. Nobody is perfect. I don't know if I'll do all of these things today. But I know when I do it, it works.

CHAPTER TWO
The 100 Rules for Being an Entrepreneur

If you Google "how to be an Entrepreneur" you get a lot of mindless clichés like "find your passion" or "think big". That's not what you are going to get here.

Again, for me, being an "entrepreneur" doesn't mean starting the next "Faceook". Or even starting any business at all. It means finding the challenges you have in your ife, and determining creative ways to overcome those challenges. However, in this chapter I focus mostly on starting a business, or at least, being an entrepreneur even in the setting of being an employee at a bigger business.

For me, I've started several businesses. As you'll see, some have succeeded, many have failed. Along the way I've compiled a list of rules that have helped me deal with every aspect of being an entrepreneur in business.

Here's the real rules:

A)   It's not fun. I'm not going to explain why it's not fun. These are rules. Not theories. I don't need to prove them. But there's a strong chance you can hate yourself throughout the process of being an entrepreneur.

B)   Try not to hire people. You'll have to hire people to expand your business. But it's a good discipline to really question if you need each and every hire.

C)   Get a customer. This seems obvious. But it's not. Get a customer before you start your business, if you can.

D)   If you are offering a service, call it a product. Oracle did it. They claimed they had a database. But if you "bought" their database they would send in a team of consultants to help you "install" the database to fit your needs. In other words, for the first several years of their existence, they claimed to have a product but they really were a consulting company. Don't forget this story.

E) It's OK to fail. Start over. Hopefully before you run out of money. Hopefully before you take in investor money.

F) Be profitable. Try to be profitable immediately. This seems obvious but it isn't. Try not to raise money. That money is expensive.

G) When raising money: if it's not easy then your idea is probably incapable of raising money.

H) The same goes for selling your company. If it's not easy, then you need to build more. Then sell.

I) Competition is good. It turns you into a killer. It helps you judge progress. It shows that other people value the space you are in.

J) Don't use a PR firm. Except maybe as a secretary. You are the PR for your company.

K) Communicate with everyone. Employees. Customers. Investors. All the time.

L) Do everything for your customers. Get them girlfriends or boyfriends. Speak at their charities. Visit their parents for Thanksgiving. Help them find other firms to meet their needs. Even introduce them to your competitors if you think a competitor can help them or if you think you are about to be fired. Always think first, "What's going to make my customer happy?"

M)   Your customer is not a company. There's a human there. What will make my human customer happy?

N)   Show up. Go to breakfast/lunch/dinner with customers.

O)   History. Know the history of your customers in every way. Company history, personal history, marketing history, investing history, etc.

P)   Micro-manage software development. Nobody knows your product better than you do. If you aren't a technical person, learn how to be very specific in your product specification so that your programmers can't say: "well you didn't say that!"

Q)   Hire local. You need to be able to see and talk to your programmers. Don't outsource to India.

R)   Sleep. Don't buy into the 20 hours a day entrepreneur myth. You need to sleep 8 hours a day to have a focused mind.

S)   Exercise. Same as above. If you are unhealthy, your product will be unhealthy.

T)   Emotionally Fit. Don't have dating problems and software development problems at the same time. VCs will smell this all over you.

U)   Pray. You need to. Be grateful where you are. And pray for success. You deserve it. Pray for the success of your customers. Heck, pray for the success of your competitors.

V)   Buy your employees gifts. Massages. Tickets. Whatever. I always imagined that at the end of each day my young, lesbian employees (for some reason, most employees at my first company were lesbian) would be calling their parents and their mom and dad would ask them: "Hi honey! How was your day today?" And I wanted them to be able to say: "It was the best!"

W)   Treat your employees like they are your children. They need boundaries. They need to be told "no!" sometimes. And sometimes you need to hit them in the face (ha ha, just kidding). But within boundaries, let them play.

X)   Don't be greedy pricing your product. If your product is good and you price it cheap, people will buy. Then you can price upgrades, future products, and future services more expensive. Which goes along with the next rule.

Y)   Distribution is everything. Branding is everything. Get your name out there, whatever it takes. The best distribution is of course word of mouth, which is why your initial pricing doesn't matter.

Z)   Don't kill yourself. It's not worth it. Your employees need you. Your children or future children need you. It seems odd to include this in a book about entrepreneurship but we're also taking about keeping it real. Most books or "rules" for entrepreneurs talk about things like "think big", "go after your dreams". But often dreams turn into nightmares. I'll repeat it again. Don't kill yourself. Call me if things get too stressful. Or more importantly, make sure you take proper medication

AA)   Give employees structure. Let each employee know how his or her path to success can be achieved. All of them will either leave you or replace you eventually. That's OK. Give them the guidelines how that might happen.

BB)   Fire employees immediately. If an employee gets "the disease" he needs to be fired. If they ask for more money all the time. If they bad mouth you to other employees. If you even think they are talking behind your back, fire them. The disease has no cure. And it's very contagious. Show no mercy. Show the employee the door.

CC)   Make friends with your landlord. If you ever have to sell your company, believe it or not, you are going to need his signature (because there's going to be a new lease owner)

DD)   Only move offices if you are so packed in that employees are sharing desks and there's no room for people to walk.

EE)   Have killer parties. But use your personal money. Not company money. Invite employees, customers, and investors. It's not the worst thing in the world to also invite off duty prostitutes or models.

FF)   If an employee comes to you crying, close the door or take him or her out of the building. Sit with him until it stops. Listen to what he has to say. If someone is crying then there's been a major communication breakdown somewhere in the company. Listen to what it is and fix it. Don't get angry at the culprit's. Just fix the problem.

GG)   At Christmas, donate money to every customer's favorite charity. But not for investors or employees.

HH)   Have lunch with your competitors. Listen and try not to talk.

II)   Ask advice a lot. Ask your customers advice on how you can be introduced into other parts of their company. Then they will help you.

JJ)   Hire your customers. Or not. But always leave open the possibility. Let it always dangle in the air between you and them. They can get rich with you. Maybe. Possibly. If they play along. So play.

KK)   On any demo, do one extra surprise thing that was not expected. Always add bells and whistles that the customer didn't pay for.

LL)   Understand the demographic changes that are changing the world. Where are marketing dollars flowing and can you be in the middle. What services do aging baby boomers need? Is the world running out of clean water? Are newspapers going to survive? Etc. Etc. Read every day to understand what is going on.

MM)   But, going along with the above rule, don't listen to the doom and gloomers that are hogging the TV screen trying to tell you the world is over. They just want you to be scared so they can scoop up all the money.

NN)   You have no more free time. In your free time you are thinking of new ideas for customers, new ideas for services to offer, new products.

OO)   You have no more free time, part 2. In your free time, think of ideas for potential customers. Then send them emails: "I have 10 ideas for you. Would really like to show them to you. I think you will be blown away. Here's five of them right now."

PP)   Talk. Tell everyone you ever knew what your company does. Your friends will help you find clients.

QQ)   Always take someone with you to a meeting. You're bad at following up. Because you have no free time. So, if you have another employee. Let them follow up. Plus, they will like to spend time with the boss.

RR)   If you are consumer focused: your advertisers are your customers. But always be thinking of new services for your consumers. Each new service has to make their life better. People's lives are better if: they become healthier, richer, or have more sex. "Health" can be broadly defined.

SS)   If your customers are advertisers: find sponsorship opportunities for them that drive customers straight into their arms. These are the most lucrative ad deals (see rule above)

TT)   No friction. The hardest it is for a consumer to sign up, the less consumers you will have. No confirmation emails, sign up forms, etc. The easier the better.

UU)   No friction, part 2. Say "yes" to any opportunity that gets you in a room with a big decision maker. Doesn't matter if it costs you money.

VV)   Sell your company two years before you sell it. Get in the offices of the potential buyers of your company and start updating them on your progress every month. Ask their advice on a regular basis in the guise of just an "industry catch-up"

WW)   If you sell your company for stock, sell the stock as soon as you can. If you are selling your company for stock it means:

    a.   The market is such that lots of companies are being sold for stock.

    b.   AND, companies are using stock to buy other companies because they value their stock less than they value cash.

c.   WHICH MEANS, that when everyone's lockup period ends, EVERYONE will be selling stock across the country. So sell yours first.

XX)   Ideas are worthless. If you have an idea worth pursuing, then just make it. You can build any website for cheap. Hire a programmer and make a demo. Get at least one person to sign up and use your service. If you want to make Facebook pages for plumbers, find one plumber who will give you $10 to make his Facebook page. Just do it.

YY)   Don't use a PR firm, part II. Set up a blog. Tell your personal stories (see "33 tips to being a better writer" below). Let the customer know you are human, approachable, and have a real vision as to why they need to use you. Become the voice for your industry, the advocate for your products. If you make skin care products, tell your customers every day how they can be even more beautiful than they currently are and have more sex than they are currently getting. Blog your way to PR success. Be honest and bloody.

ZZ)   Don't save the world. If your product sounds too good to be true, then you are a liar.

AAA)   Frame the first check. I'm staring at mine right now.

BBB)   No free time, part 3. Pick a random customer. Find five ideas for them that have nothing to do with your business. Call them and say, "I've been thinking about you. Have you tried this?"

CCC)   No resale deals. Nobody cares about reselling your service. Those are always bad deals.

DDD)   Your lawyer or accountant is not going to introduce you to any of their other clients. Those meetings are always a waste of time.

EEE)   Celebrate every success. Your employees need it. They need a massage also. Get a professional masseuse in every Friday afternoon. Nobody leaves a job where there is a masseuse.

FFF)   Sell your first company. Don't take any chances. You don't need to be Mark Zuckerberg. Sell your first company as quick as you can. You now have money in the bank and a notch on your belt. Make a billion on your next company.

GGG)   Pay your employees before you pay yourself.

HHH)   Give equity to get the first customer. If you have no product yet and no money, then give equity to a good partner in exchange for them being a paying customer. Note: don't blindly give equity. If you develop a product that someone asked for, don't give them equity. Sell it to them. But if you want to get a big distribution partner whose funds can keep you going forever, then give equity to nail the deal.

III)   Don't worry about anyone stealing your ideas. Ideas are worthless anyway. It's OK to steal something that's worthless.

Questions from Readers

Question: You say no free time but you also say keep emotionally fit, physically fit, etc. How do I do this if I'm constantly thinking of ideas for old and potential customers?

Answer: It's not easy or everyone would be rich.

Question: if I get really stressed about clients paying, how do I get sleep at night?

Answer: medication

Question: how do I cold-call clients?

Answer: email them. Email 40 of them. It's OK if only 1 answers. Email 40 a day but make sure you have something of value to offer.

Question: how can I find cheap programmers or designers?

Answer: if you don't know any and you want to be cheap: use scriptlance.com, elance.com, or craigslist. But don't hire them if they are from another country. You need to communicate with them even if it costs more money.

Question: should I hire programmers?

Answer: first…freelance. Then hire.

Question: what if I build my product but I'm not getting customers?

Answer: develop a service loosely based on your product and offer that to customers. But I hope you didn't make a product without talking to customers to begin with?

Question: I have the best idea in the world, but for it to work it requires a lot of people to already be using it. Like Twitter.

Answer: if you're not baked into the Silicon Valley ecosystem, then find distribution and offer equity if you have to. Zuckerberg had Harvard. MySpace had the fans of all the local bands they set up with MySpace pages. I (in my own small way) had Thestreet.com when I set up Stockpickr.com

Question: I just lost my biggest customer and now I have to fire people. I've never done this before. How do I do it?

Answer: one on meetings. Be Kind. State the facts. Say you have to let people go and that everyone is hurting but you want to keep in touch because they are a great employee. It was an honor to work with them and when business comes back you hope you can convince them come back. Then ask them if they have any questions. Your reputation and the reputation of your company are on the line here. You want to be a good guy. But you want them out of your office within 15 minutes. It's a termination, not a negotiation. This is one reason why it's good to start with freelancers.

Question: I have a great idea. How do I attract VCs?

Answer: build the product. Get a customer. Get money from customer. Get more customers. Build more services in the product. Get VC.

Question: I want to build a business day trading.

Answer: bad idea

Question: I want to start a business but don't know what my passion is:

Answer: skip to the chapter: "How to be the luckiest person alive". Do the Daily Practice. Within six months your life will be completely different.

Question: I want to leave my job but I'm scared.

Answer: same as above question. The Daily Practice turns you into a healthy Idea Machine. Plus luck will flow in from every direction.

Final rule: Things change. Every day. The title of this book, for instance, says "100 Rules". But I gave 74 rules (including the Q&A). Things change midway through. Be ready for it every day. In fact, every day figure out what you can change just slightly to shake things up and improve your product and company.

Throughout the rest of this book I have examples, ideas, rules, etc. In fact, it adds up to a lot more than 100 rules. I leave the funniest and most interesting rules for the chapters ahead. Many of the rules above are repeated in the chapters ahead but use this chapter as a cheat sheet. And if, after reading this book, you can think of more rules for me, than email me and I'll add them. That's the beauty of having an e-book. I can change this thing anytime I want.

CHAPTER THREE

The Woman Who Peed on her Husband

and Other Stories of Stress

"I bet people have committed suicide while starting a company" – Jason Raznick

My biggest regret: that I spent all of 2002 pacing around, stressed out of my mind, stressed over every trade, over every little downtick or uptick in my bank account, over whether or not I was going to be able to sell my Ground Zero-based apartment, over whether or not I was going to go dead broke with one kid in the family and another on the way. I'll never have that year back. I slept in a bedroom by myself so it would be easy for me to wake up and pace in the middle of the night or wander around outside. I lived in a constant state of fear. I wish I could have that year back, even if it could be tacked onto the last year of my life.

I was starting a new business: trading for hedge funds. But at the moment I had only one client and mostly I was trading my own meager amount of money that was dwindling fast under the mounting expenses I was accumulating.

Another time: 2 years later, things had already worked out from 2002. But now I needed them to work out again. I was helping an investor of mine sell his company and I would benefit from it. He had just finished telling me on the phone about how his wife peed on him the night before. **When you have a big investor you sort of have to listen to everything he says and just say: "Wow, cool."** His wife, 20 years younger than him, blonde, then grabbed the phone from him and said: "he should NOT have just told you that" and then gave the phone back to him, neither confirming nor denying. He then said to me: "I should ask for $60 million, not $40 million for my business."

Why did he say this? **Just a few months earlier he couldn't get $10 million for his little mental health business,** and now my partner and I had gotten him an offer for $40 million (for his mental health hospital for kids). How we got him an extra $30 million (**cash,** I will add) will be the subject of another story, titled, "how to make a man $40 million who is regularly peed on by his wife". I got stressed then. That night I couldn't sleep. I needed this deal to go through. I once again had that familiar feeling of the blood going through my body. I could feel every pulse. I felt I could slow my heartbeat down to zero, and then I would be dead. I was lying in my youngest daughter's bed, because both my daughters slept upstairs with their mother. So, as was usually the case back then, I slept in a pink bed surrounded by Barbie dolls, stressed out of my mind. Until I would pace again at 4 in the morning.

The next day I called my investor, "put your wife back on the phone." His wife got back on the phone. I said: "imagine that a teenage girl commit's suicide in your hospital. Your value is now $0. And that can happen any day. Also, imagine having to do for the rest of your life the job you just did yesterday." The man's wife had cleaned shit off the walls of a room where a patient had decided to do a painting with his excrement. So now we have shit, pee, $40 million, etc. in two paragraphs. She conferred with my investor after that and he stopped asking for the $60 million. They closed on $40 million for their hospital a month later. But that's another story.

Let's get back to 2002 for a second. As I've mentioned I needed my house sold. But until then, the stress was unbelievable. And then I had a second child born. So now

I was going broke, I was stressed out of my mind. Worldcom went bankrupt (I owned shares), and my new baby couldn't sleep at 2 in the morning unless I literally ran with her from one end of the house to the other. I would take long walks completely circling ground zero. This was going on for an entire year. Nothing helped. I was stressed out of my mind.

One time I tried to get a loan but the loan officer sort of looked at me and my situation and said: "we can't do this type of loan at this time." Why not? I only wanted a million or so. Why couldn't they lend it to me? But I never got an answer. Maybe if I had worn a tie.

Meanwhile, other people I had vaguely bumped into in the street years earlier were calling me asking if THEY could borrow money from me. As a collective, we all needed a little more money or we were all going broke. It wasn't a good situation to be in. Sometimes Ylon would come over and we'd play backgammon. He had just sold his apartment. "Dude," he said, "I have more money than you!"

So my biggest regret: why did I worry at all? It all worked out in the end. I could've spent the entire year just relaxing and enjoying my apartment, my new little baby, I could've read books, written a novel, started an Internet business. Instead, I wasted so much time and energy being anxious. The stress took years off my life. I can't even imagine physically having that stress again. Stress is related to cancer, heart disease, strokes, alzheimers, inflammation of the body.

Fortunately, I am the expert now in stress. I have a PhD in stress. I've lost all my money, I've fought hard to make money back, I've had people die on me, I've built businesses that have failed, I've built and sold businesses. I know stress.

When you are experiencing stress, follow this advice. Or die:

- **Be Grateful**. In 2003, if I was nervous about a trade I'd go at about 7 in the morning to the church across the street from where I lived. I'm Jewish and I've spent time meditating, but I had never prayed. But in 2003 I prayed. When you pray the key is to lean down, because then your body knows you are being humble. And then be thankful for what you have. Think of all the things you are grateful for. Just do this for five minutes. It's the easiest meditation. Then ask for anything you want.

- **Write**. This is not joke. If you don't write every day your idea muscle atrophies very quickly. And it takes months to rebuild. Here is what I do: I go to webrestaurantsupplies.com. I buy 100 waiter pads for $10. 10 cents a pad. I then fill 3 pages of ideas a day. At least. This stretches your mind. Make lists of ideas. Lists of new potential clients. Lists of emails you have to send. List of articles you want to write. Businesses you want to start (with specifics how to start it), lists of reasons you love your wife or kids. But you have to stretch your mind. FEEL the stretch. It hurts. But you have to write every day. What I find is, things start to happen if you do this for a month or so.

- **Play games**. In avoidance of the "get ready for school" routine that occurred in my house every morning at 6 in the morning I used to escape the house before everyone woke up and play scrabble with my cohorts every morning at the local cafe, (The Foundry, in Cold Spring). I memorized all the two letter words. I memorized all the "q" words with no "u". I memorized the several hundred or so easy 7 letter words (my favorite, that I was actually able to use, "etesian" and it was of course challenged and I won). This kept my mind off of my stresses and put that energy to better use.

• **Basketball**. At 5am, when the sun was rising I'd go out to the local basketball court in a field right next to the Hudson River. I'd shoot baskets until I was sweating profusely (about 45 seconds). It's good to sweat. Releases toxins.

• **Swing in a swing set**. There was a local children's playground a few blocks away. After basketball I would swing. Your brain sit's in a sea of cerebellum fluid. When you swing, that fluid swirls all around. Your brain doesn't stress then. It says, "wheeee!" No matter how old you are.

• **Go to a museum**. In 2002, in the afternoons sometimes I'd got a museum. You can easily get lost in someone else's creativity. In 2008, when the financial world was collapsing at the same time my marriage was collapsing I used to go the museum "Dia". They would have these several hundred foot long exhibitions. I could disappear for hours in those. And then sit in the cafe reading books about the artists. When it was dark I would go home, my mind awash in all the genius and creativity I had witnessed.

• **Friends**. I would love to take walks with friends that had nothing to do with the markets. People I could just talk to.

• **Comics**. I had about ten boxes of comics packed away from when I was a kid. Reading them would remind me of the stories that I loved so much when I was younger. I never knew stress when I was a kid. So it was good to be reminded of those times.

• **Sleep**. I never slept more than 3 or 4 hours at a time. Sleeping for 8 hours reduces stress. Several times I would try a routine sleeping from 4-8 in the morning and 4-8 at night. So I would get in my 8 hours but it would be irregular. It worked in a grad school but was hard to work as an adult. But you need 8 hours to be healthy and avoid stress.

• **Charity**. A couple of times I folded envelopes for "City Harvest" a charity in the city. I had a flirtatious thing going on with the other envelope folder. Charity, when done right, reduces stress. I wasn't necessarily doing it right. I wanted to brag about how stressed I was.

• **Delegating**. If you could hire people and get them to do what you are stressed about, this quickly reduces all stress. When you are building a company, the key is to know when to hire that first secretary, that first project manager, that first programmer. Once you break that hiring virginity, the rest is easy, and life is better. Until you have to meet payroll. But that's another story.

• **No TV**. TV is all stress. If you are serious about reducing stress and making your life better, no TV.

• **No drinking**. Drinking is a depressant. At the end of the day, we want to be happy. Not depressed.

• **Light dinner**. You know that feeling when you've had a heavy dinner? Like steak, fries, dessert, wine snack later while watching TV. And then sleep. And then how you feel the next day? That won't help you make your life better.

• **Shower**. It feels good to be clean. I've gone a week or two without showering. Nobody around me was happy with this. And I wouldn't change my clothes. I'd walk up and down Main Street in the town I lived in, a half beard on my face, unclean, an earpiece in my ear so I can talk to my business partner, and I'd be muttering and gesturing since we were usually in intense conversations about our favorite topic: money, and people would actually call my house and wonder if medical attention was needed. Better to shower in the morning to be fresh for the day, and shower at night, to clean away the grime of the day.

• **Teeth**. Similar with brushing teeth. After every meal and before you go to sleep and when you wake up. How come? A) avoids bad breath. B) avoids infections. An infection in your teeth can hit your brain or heart with you realizing it. Then you are in trouble!

• **Clean desk**. Some people are proud of a cluttered desk. It means they are working hard. But cluttered desk equals cluttered mind. I'm not an organized person by nature. But I always feel better when I have a clean desk. Worst case: hire someone to come over and clean your desk every few days.

• **Lists**. List the things you did yesterday. Even small things. Include all emails you send and phone calls you made. You did more than you thought.

• **By 8am** you should have a list of small to-dos you need to accomplish today. Send out 10 emails that all advance your career by noon today. 10 thank-yous or 10 "can I help" emails. You'll feel you accomplished a lot on the day. This works.

• **Quit**. If you are still stressed, think of something drastic to do with your life. Quit everything you are doing. At least entertain the idea - what else can you do? You might not be ready or capable of making a big change -yet- but start the "quit muscle" thinking of what you can do.

• **Fly a kite**. It's different. Nobody can call you while you fly a kite. You're looking at the sky the whole time the kite is in the air. You have to run to get the kite going. You have to focus to get the kite unraveled. It's the perfect meditation. It's like yoga. And then when you are sitting there watching the kite you have to remain completely focused or it will fall.

• **Make a blog**: "10 things I love about my wife". Go to blogger right now. Make a new blog. Come up with 10 things you love about your wife/husband/girlfriend/boyfriend/children. This will take ten minutes. Use Google images to come up with a fun image for each item. Surprise her.

• **Don't talk to people who are stressing you out**. You need a vacation from them. The airplane is going down, You need to put the gas mask on yourself first even if means your kid is suffering from a painful suffocation.

• **Read a spiritual text**. I made sure I did this every day. Here are some go-to texts. You only need to read a page or two. The Tao Te Ching. Anything by Chuang Tzu, Quotes of Buddha. The Bible. Pema Chodron's books. Karen Armstrong's books on the Bible.

• **Help someone with their problems**. Even though you might be stressed, sometimes we find the ability to dig deep when someone we feel compassionately about is having a problem. That ability to dig deep is hard and is also a muscle that needs to be exercised. Use it or lose it!

I was in the room when my investor got the $41 million cash wired into his account. He was so happy. His entire life had just changed and the lives of his descendants. Everyone was smiling. The wife forgot to thank me but that's OK. She would never have to clean shit off walls again, My friend said let's talk tomorrow and drove off. Over the next year he became very good at golf. The lawyers and accountants all drove off. My car service was late so I was standing in the parking spot by myself. The sun went down and it was dark. I had made some money on the deal also. Once again everything had worked out. Once again all the stress was for naught. Once again I had wasted about five months worrying.

I was scared, though. **Because I'm an addict**. And I knew the next morning there would be new things to stress about. And so I felt sad because I knew something was wrong with me. That no matter what good things were happening I had to find something to worry about. I took a deep breath and closed my eyes. Sometimes, tomorrow is just another day. Thank God it's today.

CHAPTER FOUR
The Wu-Tang Clan, Hitler, and My First Year as an Entrepreneur

The first day I became an entrepreneur I cried. I had already been running a company, Reset, on the side while I worked at HBO fulltime. Our clients at Reset included American Express, Con Edison, various divisions within Time Warner, BMG, Universal, and of course, HBO. I couldn't keep conducting business from my cubicle. My boss, his boss, his boss, his boss, and his boss, were already suspicious of me. I had a cubicle in the HBO building and it was crowded with contracts from their competitors.

When I arrived at Reset fulltime the first call I made was to Steve. He had told me two weeks earlier the Wu-tang-clan wanted us to do websites for all of their back CDs. And we'd do websites for every other group that Loud Records had. I ran the numbers in my head. Maybe it would be $900,000 worth of work. The Wu-tang-clan was into chess and boxing and they wanted me specifically to help them. They had an album called "The Mystery of Chess-boxing". It was my favorite album at the time because what did I care.

"Forget the wu-tang-clan," he told me on the phone that first day. "They are scumbags. Why would you want to do business with them?" Suddenly it was my fault for wanting something. Just the other day it was a done deal. I was practically in the Wu-tang-clan. They "loved" me. A year later Ol Dirty Bastard was telling me the best thing he had ever done at 3 in the morning was sit in the mountains listening to owls go "ooo….ooo". But that was ancient history that hadn't yet happened. And now he's dead.

Something had gone horribly wrong. In the music business, person A pays person B who pays person C. who then somehow returns the favor. But it's a game of operator where money is whispered into everyone's ear before being passed along. By the end of the telephone chain, someone's out of business, everyone's paid money, and everyone is angry at everyone else. The deal was over.

I made a few more calls but nobody would take my call. I wasn't at HBO anymore. I went out for a pizza on 17th St and 7th Avenue. It was summer and hot. I had thought it would make sense to wear a jacket and tie but that was like a joke. Who wears a tie to call the Wu-tang clan? It was the best pizza I had ever tasted. But I cried a bit when I realized how radically I had changed my life without having any idea of what I was doing.

This was in a world before venture capitalists. If you had a business, you needed to make money. You needed to call people and sell them all day long. At night you needed to lie awake figuring out how you were going to pay the people you promised the world to. Because business is religion and your employees are your followers. There were no parties or "summit's", then, for founders. You trashed your competitors to everyone you could. Nobody was your friend and we all worked within a five block radius of each other centering around 6th Avenue and 17th street.

Several survival techniques I learned:

•   Hire freelancers so you could always fire them when the revenues invariably dip.

•   Your old customers are your best new customers. Offer more and more services to them. It's hard for them to say no.

• Say "yes" to everything when you are selling. Do anything to add to your client list. The services business for a service that nobody understands (web development back then) is enormously profitable but you need your foot in the door. Then you figure out the profit.

• Corollary to above: Make it as easy as possible for them to say yes. Offer to do stuff for free until they say yes.

• Do favors for as many people as you can. You can't give bribes but if you spend your entire life doing favors for clients then eventually someone will repay the favor. Give clients advice on their business. Advise clients how to get promoted. Find people jobs, girlfriends, send enormous gift packages at Christmas (or birthdays, Valentine's Day, or just for the heck of it), do things for their charities,

• Fire any employee instantly who has a negative attitude. Negativity is a cancer. It can't be cured (by you) and it spreads quickly through the rest of your company.

• Ask clients for advice about your business. Make them feel involved, almost like owners, without giving them equity. New clients are your best salespeople because they want their peers to help them feel justified in their decisions.

• Look for the half-chewed leftovers from your competitors that are growing faster than you. Their older clients will begin to hate them.

• Bring in a professional masseuse one day a week for your employees. It costs nothing and when they are working for you at 1 in the morning on a Saturday night they'll be thankful they work in such a great work environment.

• Never do a deal where someone else is re-selling your services. Nobody else cares about selling your product/services.

• Follow up with potential clients by asking them to dinner or breakfast. Pick the nicest place. Pick up the tab. Ask them about their love life.

• Never listen to anyone who says, "I want to make you rich". They don't.

• If someone steers you the wrong way once, never listen to them again. It's a waste of time.

• Over promise and over-deliver. But only the first time.

• If someone says, "I'm taking a big chance by hiring you," assume that you'll never do business with them again and get paid as quickly as possible.

• If a client says, "I'd rather have this conversation in our offices", don't go there. Never go there again.

• If someone wants to buy your company, immediately look for a better offer. Don't accept the bulk of pay in earn-outs,

"Power", who claimed he was representing the Wu Tang Clan, said to me: "you're one of us now." A year later, to the day, the son of the German doctor who killed Hitler bought my company. But that's another story.

CHAPTER FIVE

How to Succeed in LA without Really Trying

She asked me if she could play. I was in a bar in a hotel in LA going over a game on a portable chessboard while waiting for Steve to arrive so we could go out for dinner. This woman sat down about two seats from me, looked over, and then challenged me to a game.

It was almost surreal because nothing like that had ever happened to me before. It was like a scene from a chess movie only nobody would ever make a movie about chess. How could I refuse? So we started the first few moves and she wasn't awful. She told me her last boyfriend was Benecio del Toro but now he wasn't calling her back. And now she was playing chess with me. The only reason I was staying at this hotel, "The Bel Age", was because that's where the TV show Beverly Hills 90210 had their prom.

Steve finally arrived and I introduced them. I want to think she seemed sad to see me leave.

We left. I was thinking I was pretty cool at that moment. Steve was like, "what the fuck!? That was a high end prostitute!"

"No way," I said, "she played chess." Somehow all the circuitry in my brain was fried. Everything was on fire.

"Man," he said, "she was a call girl. The last time I was in this hotel I saw [owner of now defunct record store chain] with prostitutes all over him. She was a call girl."

Maybe it was the thought that she was "high end" made me feel a little better about it? I don't know.

Steve and I went to dinner where we met up with a guy who had just gotten out of jail. Steve and I were tiny Jews in LA. This guy was the opposite of that. He was the size of three bathroom stalls put together. He said over dinner, "when [jailed famous hip hop mogul] gets out of jail, Snoop better be in hiding. I give him 30 days before Snoop is dead." As we were walking out of dinner, he said to me: "I really like what you do. Can I stop by and hang out in your office next time I'm in New York?"

What can you say to that?

On the way back to the hotel I ask Steve if he's going to pay his bills anytime soon. His company owed me $80k. I had a payroll of 40 people I had to make. Steve was in charge of Internet stuff for [famous record label]. "Why are you always asking me that?" Steve said, "Don't you trust me? And your guy Adrian was threatening my secretary today. Tell him to back the fuck off or I'll never fucking pay you." Now I had to apologize because I never did business back then with a contract so I had nobody to sue. It was all "relationships".

We stopped off at a bar where the owner of Steve's record label was hanging out in a booth with two beautiful girls. He was a billionaire known for having multiple women around all the time. Steve introduced us and said to him: "you guys would get along. James plays chess." And the guy said, "Oh yeah? I just sponsored the World Chess Championship with Kasparov" but then turned away and started kissing one of the girls.

At the bar was [famous comedian] whose TV show I had just done the website for. I was feeling shy but Steve laughed and encouraged me to go over and introduce myself. I went over to him and said: "Hey, sorry for interrupting but I'm a big fan. I just wanted to mention that I just did your website for your TV show." He looked at me, squinted for a second or two and said, very, very slowly, "who. are. you.?" and then everyone around him laughed.

The next day I went over to UTA, the big talent agency that represented, among others, Jim Carrey. "We love your stuff," they said, "we want to do something big with Jim Carrey. It has to be really really big." I threw out some ideas. "We LOVE that. Let's do it!" One guy said, "you should come with us to this party tonight."

But I was unsure if I had other plans. An hour later, when my other plans canceled I called one of them and said, "hey, I can go to that party," and he said, "oh, we made other plans but we LOVED your stuff. Call us next time you are in town and we'll do something." I never spoke to him again despite repeated calls when I got back to New York.

For one thing, I wear sweaters. And I don't drive. People in LA don't get either of those things. I tend to look different and stand out because I'm walking on the side of the road a lot.

I had breakfast the next morning with a guy who invented the kind of pen where it changes according to how your fingers press it. He was in his late 50s but was tan and fit. He wanted to make a website to sell his pens. He ordered pancakes and French toast but had only one bite of each. "I like to test things," he said, "for my restaurant. You should stop by." I had done a website once for a movie he produced. Headless Body In Topless Bar. "I lost a half million on that movie. You know what that's like?" I said no.

He opened up his cellphone. "This is technology. This is where it's going." He had a speaker on the cellphone and called someone. A sleepy sounding woman answered,

"Hello?" "Hello, baby," he said, "Just showing my new friend this new technology." Then he snapped it shut. "I don't like you," he said to me. "You didn't comb your hair before you came to meet me and you're disheveled. You should clean up a little if you want to do business with me."

Later that day I had lunch with a friend of mine who had moved to LA a year earlier. She was now a Pilates instructor for [famous female comedian]. "I love it here," she said. "It's so much healthier." I felt bad it never worked out with us (and I never had a chance) but she was married now and she really did look happy and healthy.

Later that night I took the red eye home. I can never sleep in planes so I try to read but I'm too tired and end up in this weird stupor while everyone sleeps in the dark around me. When I landed I went straight into the office. It was early and the sun was just creeping out. I could see the smoke from my breath in the cold air when I got into the cab. My sister was already at the office when I got there. "Hey!" she said, "how was LA?"

It was awesome.

CHAPTER SIX
Do Not Send Your Kids to College

Student loan debt is now greater than credit card debt and homeowner debt. For the first time ever we are graduating a generation of indentured servants!

The American Religion has told us we need to send our kids to college in order for our lineage to reach some form of stable happiness. This is a myth and blind adherence to this myth will infringe on our ultimate happiness.

Instead, its time to look at the reality and think of the alternatives. I get strong reactions on this topic. Religion is a touchy subject for many people. But at the end of your life there's only you and nobody else to question the decisions you've made.

The average tuition cost is approximately $16,000 per year. Plus assume another $10,000 in living costs, books, etc. $26,000 in total for a complete cost of $104,000 in a 4 year period. Some people choose to go more expensive by going to a private college and some people choose to go a little cheaper by going public but this is an average. Also, a huge assumption is that is just for a 4-year period. According to the Department of Education, only 54% of undergraduates graduate within 6 years. So for the 46% that don't graduate, or take 10 years to graduate, this is a horrible investment. But let's assume your children are in the brilliant first half who finish within six years (and hopefully within four).

Is it worth it? First, let's look at it completely from a monetary perspective. Over the course of a lifetime, according to CollegeBoard, a college graduate can be expected to earn $800,000 more than his counterpart that didn't go to college. $800,000 is a big spread and it could potentially separate the haves from the have-nots. But who has and who doesn't?

If I took that $104,000 and I chose to invest it in a savings account that had interest income of 5% per year I'd end up with an extra $1.4 million dollars over a 50 year period. A full $600,000 more. That $600,000 is a lot of extra money an 18 year old could look forward to in her retirement. I also think the $800,000 quoted above is too high. Right now most motivated kids who have the interest and resources to go to college think it's the only way to go if they want a good job. If those same kids decided to not go to college my guess is they would quickly close the gap on that $800,000 spread.

There are other factors as well. I won't be spending $104,000 per child when my children, ages 12and 9 decide to go to college. College costs have historically gone up much faster than inflation. Since 1978, cost of living has gone up three-fold. Medical costs, much to the horror of everyone in Congress, has gone up six-fold. And college education has gone up a whopping tenfold. This is beyond the housing bubble, the stock market bubble, any bubble you can think of.

So how can people afford college? Well, how has the US consumer afforded anything? They borrow it, of course. The average student now graduates with a $23,000 debt burden. Up from $13,000 12 years ago. Last year, student borrowings totaled $75 billion, up 25% from the year before. If students go on to graduate degrees such as law degrees they can see their debt burden soar to $200,000 or more. And the easy borrowing convinces colleges that they can raise prices even more.

8 More Reasons Parents Should Not Send Their Kids to College

1. People say: Kids learn to be socialized at college. Are you kidding me? I'm going to spend $100-200k a year so my kids can learn how to make friends with other people their age? Let me tell you about how your kids will be socialized in college and you know this to be true:

> ——-Your kid should put a dime in a glass jar every time he or she has sex in his first year of college. After the first year of college, he or she should take a dime out every time they have sex. They will never empty that jar. I might be exaggerating (it's hard for me to do the math on numbers in four digits like this when I look back at my own experience). So assume that's step #1 on the socialization of our children in college.

> ——Do the same exercise above with the dimes but replace "sex" with "vomit". That's part #2 with the socialization.

> ——You can also do the above exercise with the dimes (give your kid lots of dimes before they say, "ok, Dad, see you LATER!" when you drop them off in the parking lot of college.) but instead of "sex" or "vomit" say "classes I will skip because of either sex or vomiting."

2. People say: Kids learn how to think in college. This argument was said to me by Kathryn Schulz, author of "Being Wrong", a good friend and author of an excellent book. But she knows more than anyone that no matter how much you think you "think", you're going to be wrong most of the time. And by the way, does it really cost several hundred thousand dollars to learn how to think?

I would argue that college is a way to avoid learning how to think. If I want to learn how to play tennis, the best thing to do is go out on a tennis court and play tennis. If I want to learn how to drive a car, I better get behind a wheel and drive. If I want to learn how to live and how to think, then the best thing to do is begin living my life and thinking my thoughts instead of still having my parents pay for my life and my professors giving me my thoughts. See below to see how I learned how to "think".

3. Statistics say: College graduates make much more money than non-college graduates. Clearly anyone who states this has failed "Statistics 101" in college. We might know correlation but we don't know cause-and-effect here. Since our generation (post-baby boomer) basically everyone goes to college except people who absolutely failed high school, then of course it makes sense that achievement-minded people make more money than individuals who are not achievement-oriented.

A better statistical study, which nobody has done, is take 2000 people who got accepted to Harvard 20 years ago, and randomly force 1000 of them to not go to college. Then, at the end of 20 years to see who made more money. My guess is that the 1000 that didn't go to Harvard would've made more money. They would've been thrown out of the nest to learn how to fly that much earlier and a 5 year head start would've made enormous difference (I say 5 years because that's the average amount of time it takes to finish college. Not 4, as many think).

4. One person said: Not everything boils down to money. Specifically, one brilliant commenter on one of my posts said, "I'd say the overwhelming majority of people don't go to college as a financial investment. They do it because they want to explore career options in an easy environment. They do it because there's a particular career they want to be (unfortunately weekend hackers don't often become doctors) they do it because they want to drink and party on the weekends. They do it because the point of life is not making money."

I'm going to be angry for the first time on this chapter, if not this entire book since its inception. What a stupid statement that is. If it's not a financial investment then why has the cost of college gone up 1000% in the same amount of time it's taken healthcare to go up 700% and inflation to go up 300%? It's a financial investment because college presidents have scammed most kids into thinking they can't get jobs without college. So they jack up the prices knowing kids will be forced to pay otherwise suffer the perceived opportunity cost of not going to college.

Also, the commenter above says "the point of life is not making money". I'd like to thank him for saying that. Otherwise i would've gone through life thinking the entire point of life was making money. I'm assuming what he really means by that statement is that it's great for kids to read books about philosophy, literature, art, history, etc. in an environment that encourages discussion among peers and experts. This is what college is truly great for.

5. **My Experience.** I think of myself as an educated person so let me tell you my own experience:

College itself was spent:

- Meeting and fooling around with girls for the first time in my life. I'm glad the banks loaned me enough money to do this. And fortunately, extreme failure and embarrassment in this arena didn't affect me at all later in life.

- learning about alcohol and the occasional recreational drug for the first time in my life

- I took an enormous amount of classes in Computer Science. None of which helped me in my first actual non-academic job. In fact, I was so bad at computers after going to both undergrad Cornell in Computer Science and graduate school at Carnegie Mellon in Computer Science that my first non-academic job (HBO) had to send me to two months of training courses at AT&T so I could learn a thing or two about how computers were used in the real world. My first task at HBO was to get some computer they gave me "onto the Internet". I ended up crashing the computer so bad they had to throw it out and I also wiped out everyone's email on that computer. I thought they were going to fire me but they just banished me for two months instead. The only way to get fired at HBO, I was told, was to stand on your boss's desk and pee on it.

- I borrowed every penny of my college education. I took courses every summer (they were cheaper and quicker then) and I took six courses a semester. I still graduated without about 30-40k in loans. It took me ten years (and selling a business) but I paid back every penny of my loans.

- On top of my courses, I worked about 40 hours a week at jobs so I could afford my expenses. My parents did not pay one dime of my expenses except for maybe my first semester of college. And for graduate school I got a full scholarship and stipend.

The way I got educated in reading, philosophy, history, art, etc. was fully on my own time. After leaving graduate school I took relatively easy jobs as a programmer on campus. I spent hours every day reading books, and then at least another hour or two a day going to the campus library and reading criticism on the books I had just finished.

This was the entirety of my liberal arts education. And it was all for free and has served me well since then. And I was actually paid while I was doing it.

If you can't read a book without being on a college campus and paying $100-200k a year for the honor of being there then you probably shouldn't be reading books anyway. Or at least wait until you learn the value of a dollar before making that extreme expense.

6. **Parents are scammed.** If you are a parent and wish to send your kids to a college then, just to summarize, here is what you are paying for:

- your kids are going to have scx 1- 5 times a day with people you probably wouldn't approve of.

- your kids are going to drink, smoke pot, probably try LSD and other drugs before you even get home

- your kids are going to cheat on most of their exams. When I first started college I wanted to be a psychologist. I read every book on psychology. In Psych 101 I got a D- on my first exam, which was graded on a curve. Apparently the other 2000 kids in the class had access to older exams which were stored at all the fraternities and the professor never changed the exams. I had to ultimately drop Psych as a major. My dad said, "why do you want to major in Psychology anyway. Girls won't like you because you won't make any money as a psychologist." I said, "but then I'll never know if the girls like me for money or not?" And he said, "Girls won't like you because you have money. They'll like you because YOU ARE THE KIND OF GUY who can make a lot of money."

- your kids are going to make connections with other like-minded individuals (people focused on drugs, socialism, sex 24 hours a day (not a bad thing), people cheating on exams, and people with rich parents who will help your kids get jobs at Goldman Sachs).

- your kids are going to think they are smarter than you almost immediately.

- while you are working 60 hours a week and borrowing money to send your kids to college, your kids will be sleeping good chunks of the day, relaxing on the weekends, and enjoying the blissful pleasures of the lazy life for another four years until the real world hits.

7. **Alternatives**

Let's look at the alternatives to college. And yes, some of these cost money. But all of these cost far less than the cost of college and, heck, your kids might learn some skills along the way that, god forbid, help them make more money later:

1) **Start a business.** There are many businesses a kid can start, particularly with the Internet. But if you always focus on the maxim, "buy low and sell high", you'll start to generate ideas.

Many people say (correctly), "well, not everyone can be an entrepreneur". It's amazing to me, also, how many times I've answered this question in writing and yet people still read the exact articles and say "well not everyone can be an entrepreneur".

First off, there's no law against being an entrepreneur. In fact, everyone can be an entrepreneur. So what they really mean is: "not everyone can be a successful entrepreneur". And as far as I know, there's no law against failure either. When someone loses a tennis match or a chess game, how do they improve? They study their loss. As anyone who has mastered any field in life knows: studying your losses is infinitely more valuable than studying your wins. I failed at my first three attempts at being an entrepreneur before I finally learned how to spell it and had a success (i.e. a company with profits that I was then able to sell).

Failure is a part of life. Better to learn it at 18 than at 23 or older when you've been coddled by ivory blankets and hypnotized into thinking success was yours for the taking. Get baptized in the river of failure as a youth so you can blossom in entrepreneurial blessings as an adult.

What do you learn when you are young and start a business (regardless of success or failure):

- you learn how to come up with ideas that will be accepted by other people

- you begin to build your bullshit detector (something that definitely does not happen in college)

- you learn how to sell your idea

- you learn how to build and execute on an idea

- you meet and socialize with other people in your space. They might not all be the same age but, let's face it, that's life as an adult. You just spent 18 years with kids your age. Grow up!

- you might learn how to delegate and manage people

- you learn how to eat what you kill, a skill also not learned by college-goers

2) **Travel the world.** Here's a basic assignment. Take $10,000 and get yourself to India. Check out a world completely different from our own. Do it for a year. You will meet other foreigners traveling. You will learn what poverty is. You will learn the value of how to stretch a dollar. You will often be in situations where you need to learn how to survive despite the odds being against you. If you're going to throw up you might as well do it from dysentery than from drinking too much at a frat party. You will learn a little bit more about eastern religions compared with the western religions you grew up with. You will learn you

aren't the center of the universe. Knock yourself out.

3) **Create art.** Spend a year learning how to paint. Or how to play a musical instrument. Or write 5 novels. Learn to discipline yourself to create. Creation doesn't happen from inspiration. It happens from perspiration, discipline, and passion. Creativity doesn't come from God. It's a muscle that you need to learn to build. Why not build it while your brain is still creating new neurons at a breathtaking rate than learning it when you are older (and for many people, too late).

4) **Make people laugh.** This is the hardest of all. Spend a year learning how to do standup-comedy in front of people. This will teach you how to write. How to communicate. How to sell yourself. How to deal with people who hate you. How to deal with the psychology of failure on a daily basis. And, of course, how to make people laugh. All of these items will help you later in life much more than Philosophy 101 will. And, by the way, you might even get paid along the way.

5) **Write a book.** Believe me, whatever book you write at the age of 18 is probably going to be no good. But do it anyway. Write a novel about what you are doing instead of going to college. You'll learn how to observe people. Writing is a meditation on life. You'll live each day, interpret it, and write it. What a great education!

6) **Work in a charity**. Plenty of charities do not require you to have a college degree. What is going to serve you better in life: taking French Literature 101 or spending a year delivering meals to senior citizens with Alzheimers, or curing

malaria in Africa. I have an answer to this. You might have a different one. Which is why I'm listing 8 alternatives here instead of just this one. And, by the way, if you do any of these items for a year, two years, maybe ten, then maybe go to college? Why not? It's your life.

7) **Master a game:** What's your favorite game? Ping pong? Chess? Poker? Learning how to master a game is incredibly hard. I've written before how to do it but let's start with the basics:

1. study the history of the game

2. study current experts on the game. videos, books, magazines, etc. Replay, or try to imitate in some way, the current masters of the game

3. Play a lot: with friends, in tournaments, at local clubs, etc.

4. take lessons from someone who has already mastered the game. This helps you to avoid bad habits and gets someone to immediately criticize your current skills.

Mastering a game builds discipline lets you socialize with other people of all ages and backgrounds but who have similar passions, and helps you to develop the instincts of a killer without having to kill anyone. Nice!

8) **Master a sport:** Probably even better than mastering a game because it's the same as all of the above but you also get in shape.

If anyone can think of any other alternatives, please list them in the comments. We only have the life we have lived. And I always sit and daydream, 'what if...', 'what if...' It's the easiest and most dangerous meditation to do: what if.

Because that wish is like a wisp of smoke that can twist and turn until we disappear along with it. But as I write this chapter I look at these alternatives with longing and I know that when I read this later I'm going to sit here quietly while the sun goes down, wondering only about 'what if'.

CHAPTER SEVEN
Wherein My Kiss Was Rejected

I was leaning in for the kiss and she put up the hand. We were 22 years old. "I can't," she said. "I'm in a tough spot in my life. I've been through some things recently and my therapist told me I can't do three things over the next year: change where I live, change my job, and change my relationship status – which is single."

Of course I believed her then. I was young and foolish and my ego required that I believe her. Now, with 20 years of further experience, and many rejections later, I realized that it was a total blow off. She just wasn't that into me. But now that I'm thinking more about it (since it's not atypical of me to dwell on 20-year old rejections) I realize that the advice this "therapist" gave is HORRIBLE advice in most situations.

In fact, if you have stress in your life, the number one thing you need to do today is SHAKE THINGS UP. When you are mugged or if a car is about to hit you, your stress hormones fire off and you FIGHT or FLIGHT. **The same thing happens when you are an entrepreneur**. You are mugged every day. Every day is a fight or fight scenario. You are constantly in a state when your need to shake things up for yourself, for your company, for your customers, or all of the above.

A) **Do something insane**. I'm going to admit something. A few years ago, it was a Thanksgiving. I was going through a separation with my then-wife. I was in a hotel by myself with nothing to do on a major holiday. I decided to do something completely insane. I went on Craigslist and advertised that I was a psychic and would help anyone with any problem. For the rest of that day I answered people's questions (telling people in advance that I couldn't see the future, or find objects, etc. but could answer any other question – like a therapist of sorts). It was fun and took me out of my body and mind for a few hours. And I actually made one or two long-term friends out of it.

B)   **Save a life**. Deep down you know you are a superhero. And in every episode of a superhero's life, there's a person that needs saving. Today's an episode. Go do it. Stay anonymous so your secret identity is protected. Everyone needs saving of some sort. Keep your eye out and you'll find who needs saving today.

C)   **Go jump in a river**. A few months ago I had a particularly stressful day. It was bad from a trading point of view and other reasons. I hadn't gone swimming in years even though I live right next to the Hudson River. So I went a few blocks from where I live where there's basically a mud beach, and I went swimming in the river for a while. It was nice and warm and made me forget about whatever was bothering me. Not everyone can just go jump in a river but certainly you can find something you haven't done in years and just go ahead and do it. For instance, find a firing range near where you live and fire some guns. About twelve years ago I did this when I was undergoing a particularly stressful time involving the sale of my first business. It was looking like the deal was not going through. Firing some rifles at a target did wonders for my stress levels.

D)   **Return some emails from 2005** that have nothing to do with anything. Sometimes I go back in my emails from several years ago and I return or follow-up on, an email from back then as if no time has passed at all. Like asking a co-worker who asked you for help in 2006 on a specific project, "Hey, do you still need help with that project. I'm available now." It's always a surprise to the person on the other end to see a response from an email they sent in

2006. You never know what could happen. I have 93,311 unread emails in my Inbox at the moment (not counting the ones in the Spam folder). I have a lot of material to work with but you never know what you could find when you go digging back through your own archives. It's like an archaeological dig. If you are the type of person who responds to all emails, then respond again to a 2005 email.

E)   **Ask someone new for coffee**. Basically, upgrade the average quality of your friends. Drop (or slow down) a friend that brings you down, and invite for coffee someone you think could be an interesting new friend. Learn something new over coffee. Imagine if you did this once a week. You'd have a pretty high quality group of friends after a short period of time. That's shaking things up.

F)   **Send your resume around**. The job market is like any other market. It has supply and demand and everything has its value. At least every two years you need to find out what your value is in the market. I'll give an example. I once worked with a very talented woman who worked in the marketing department of a major television network. She was unhappy in her job so I arranged a dinner between her and the head of a new but growing ad agency. The ad agency woman loved my friend but: "She's too inbred". She had been at the TV network for 17 years and the ad agency would've been too worried she couldn't adapt. Remain adaptable, and at the very least, keep careful track of your value in the marketplace. You do this by sending the resume around and making sure you get at least one offer, or at the very least, some good advice.

G)   **Unusual Love**. Follow the 32 Unusual Ways to Love Ourselves:

http://earthyogi.blogspot.com/2010/08/32-unusual-ways-to-love-ourselves.html

H)   **Take an artist's holiday**. Do this by yourself. Go to a museum, look at paintings, and think about art and what artistic things you can do. This is easy if you live in a major city. If you don't, then go to any close city that has art galleries or someplace where you can spend a few hours milling around looking at creativity in action. Oh, and do this on a weekday instead of a weekend. Going to a museum on a weekend is like going to a children's party at a public swimming pool. Someone's going to pee on you.

I)   **Make a list of things one can do to de-stress**. Trust me this works.

J)   **Forgive and Forget**. Find one person to forgive. I have a lot of people that I feel have done me wrong. People I've done favors for, people I've made money for, people who I have really helped who have then in some way or other then treated me in a way I didn't like. And I hold grudges. Pick one of them at random and forgive them. Really mean it. It will make life a little easier. One less person to think about.

K)   **Clean your desk**. Throw out as many things as possible. I know the whole "hoarders" movement seems to be catching on in reality TV. But I find when I throw out as much stuff as possible, even things that I thought were desperately important or sentimental to me, I feel a little better.

L)   **Beg**. If you live in a major city, lie down in the sidewalk for a little while with a sign that says you're hungry and need some money. Believe me, this makes enough money for a McDonalds meal, which comes in handy because after a while of begging you can get hungry.

M)   **Unusual Concentration**. Pay attention to the 32 Unusual Ways to Practice Concentration. See Claudia's blog (www.EarthYogi.blogspot.com).

N)   **The "I Did" List**. You know how a lot of people make a "to-do" list? To-do lists are sometimes stressful for me. How are you going to get all that stuff done if you are stressed out? Even better, make an "I did" list. List all the things you did that day that were productive. It's probably bigger than you think. Do it again tomorrow also. It will improve. On days where I feel like I did nothing it's amazing to me how many things I did once I make the "I did" list.

O)   **Wear all white clothes**, or as close as possible to white. It worked for Mark Twain when he lost his wife and daughter. He switched to an all-white tuxedo wardrobe and it worked for him.

P)   **The 60 Second Meditation**. I'll be honest, suggesting meditation or exercise to people might be an accurate thing to do on this list (both reduce stress) but it's not overly realistic. People have a hard time setting aside a few moments to do either. Here are some meditations that are fun, take only a few minutes, and will reduce stress:

> 1.   Make a list in your head of all the people in your life you are grateful for. Only takes a few minutes, drastically reduces stress.

> 2.   Mentioned above, but think of one person you really hate. Now, truly and sincerely wish him the best in your head. This person is just trying to get through life also. Maybe they've lost some money, or maybe they are lonely. But there is some suffering that caused them to do the things they did. Wish him or her the best. And mean it.

3.   This borders on psychosis, but pretend you are Jesus, or Buddha. Really visualize it. You are the son of God. Or maybe you are Luke Skywalker, completely giving yourself over to The Force. Now, you know God has a mission for you, and just like that guy in Mission Impossible (the TV show, not the movies) you have to listen to that tape and do whatever it says. God is on the tape. Then it explodes (stressful) and you have to do what it says.

4.   Tense every muscle in your body for 5 seconds. Tense as much as you can. Then relax. Feels better, right?

5.   When you are walking around in the city, if you are anything like me you probably hate most of the people who you pass, even if you don't know them or have never seen them before. Catch yourself doing that. Try the reverse. Try liking all of them. Not in a patronizing way (i.e. don't give anyone sympathy). But try to really like them.

Q)   **Introduce two people to each other**. It doesn't matter the reason. Just write to both and say: "you two should definitely meet." Think about it this way, the most successful businesses in history did this. Nobody goes to Google for its content. Google just introduces people to each other. You become Google or Yahoo when you are the guy in the middle. Most companies hate to link out to other sites. But that's all wrong. When you are in the middle, you become the go-to person. You're the person people go to when THEY need to shake things up.

R)   **A 25 Hour Day**. Not every job or life situation will allow this. But try it if you can: Stay up an extra hour every day, but still sleep 8 hours (or whatever your normal sleep schedule is). In other words, unlike most mere mortals, who are living a 24 hour day, you are living a 25 hour day. Do it for at least a month (or 24 days) so you can see how it feels for a full cycle. Strange things happen when you live the 25 hour day. Trust me. A variation on this is to split your sleep cycle in half. Sleep 4-8 in the morning and 4-8 in the afternoon. Still 8 hours but…different.

S)   **Do All of the Above**. In fact, you can do all of the above in a single day. Try the "Shake Things Up" day where do you all of the things suggested above in a 25 hour period.

CHAPTER EIGHT
The Easiest Way to Succeed as an Entrepreneur

I was the worst pizza delivery guy. Fraternity guys would chase after me as I was peeling out of their driveways after a delivery. Why? The sauce and cheese fell all to one side. I couldn't help it. I also never got tips. Wende, my partner in our restaurant delivery business, always got tips. But she was beautiful, blonde, great smile, had personality, etc. And I secretly loved her. I couldn't compete. I always hoped I would deliver to a frat party where all the girls were running around naked. But that never happened.

We also started a debit card for college kids. From the first day we were open for business we had college kids signing up for our card (there were no credit cards for kids then). And anyone who had our debit card could order food from the 20 or so restaurants in town and we'd deliver, but with a 25% markup.

I loved delivering food because it gave me twenty, or even forty minute breaks from my girlfriend. We were having troubles at the time. I'd sometimes stop the car between deliveries and just read. I was a screwed up 19 year old then. Now I'm only a mildly-screwed up 43 year old.

I've had seven startups since then. And some profitable exit's. And another 20 or so that I've funded.

When I think "entrepreneur" I think Mark Cuban or Larry Page or Steve Jobs. I don't usually think of myself. In part because I feel shame that after all of these startups I don't have a billion dollars. Many startups fail. But I've had a few successes as well. Successes in a startup make you feel immortal.

I was going to make this chapter: "the 12 rules to being a good entrepreneur" and I outlined the 12 rules that have consistently worked for me. But rule #1 is taking up 1500 words already. Tim Sykes tells me I need to break these chapters up more. So this one rule is going to take up the whole chapter. But, for me, this is the most important rule.

The MOST IMPORTANT RULE: Have a customer before you start your business. This is a corollary of the phrase, "ideas are a dime a dozen".

There is another corollary: lazy is best. If you have to work for two years before one dollar of revenue comes into business then that's too much work. I'm lazy so I like money coming in with as little work as possible. Mark Zuckerberg, of course, is different. He put in years of work before dollar one of revenue came in. But we're different people.

In about twenty minutes I'm going to go to the local café here, The Foundry, and bring a pad, order a coffee and muffin, and write down ideas for businesses. Then I'll probably throw the piece of paper out. Because ideas are useless. They are just practice to keep your idea muscle in shape. [See Chapter on "How to be the luckiest person alive].

FAKE RULE: People say, "Execution is important". That's not really true either. **Execution is useless**. It's a commodity. The only thing that's important is money. You get money by having a customer. You get a customer by satisfying a need that's so important to them they would be willing to pay for it. If you have a customer that's willing to pay you money, then execution becomes a lot easier. Life as an entrepreneur is hard. Why make it harder for yourself?

I like stability as much as I like taking risks. So for me, I need a customer. It's a matter of how much risk you want to take. In a post at jamesaltucher.com I suggest reasons why people need to quit their jobs and jump into the abyss. If a customer happens to be waiting for you in the abyss then you won't be lonely there. Loneliness is bad for a startup.

Example: How Stockpickr Started

Tom Clarke, the CEO of Thestreet.com called me up in mid-2006. He wanted to meet and brainstorm ideas with me. So I had about two weeks to prepare. I called up a development firm in India. MySpace had just been acquired by NewsCorp so I sketched out what I considered the "MySpace of Finance". I threw in every idea from my own trading.

In other words, I wanted to create a site that I would use as a professional trader and so I knew other traders would benefit from it. And, I had a theory about making a quality financial site that basically had no news in it. I'm going to be blunt: 99% of financial news is useless and misinformed and misleading, if not outright lying. My ideas for the site were purely based on my own ten years' experience as a professional trader. In fact, I had just turned down working for a multi-billion dollar hedge fund based on a specific strategy I had. Instead, I implemented that strategy within Stockpickr.com.

Within a week, for free (because I told the company in India that I would be building the site with them if they sent back good screenshots, which was true), the company sent me back screenshots. I met with Tom and told him, "I'm almost done with the site. Here it is." (I exaggerated) And I showed him the screenshots. I had set up meetings with Yahoo and AOL as well to discuss them so it wasn't a stretch to say, "I'm also talking to Yahoo and AOL." Nobody wants to be the first customer, so you have to create the aura of many customers.

And so he said: "why are you talking with them? You've been with us forever. Let's do this together." So we negotiated right there. I said: "great, how about you guys take 10% of the company and put all your extra ads on all of our pages and let me link from every article back to Stockpickr.com (the name of the company)."

He said: "I thought we were partners. Let's do it 50-50." So right away, **I had given up 50% of the company**. Most people I spoke to thought this was a horrible idea. In fact, one of my employees quit because I did this: but giving 50% of your company away is often better than giving 10% of your company away. When you give 50% of the company away, your partner is obligated to follow through and be a real partner. He can never forget about you. It's also always a good thing when the most popular person in financial media, Jim Cramer, was also a 50% partner in my business since he was the founder of Thestreet.com. If you can get the top person in your field to take equity, you're golden from day one. Again, it's all about making life easy. With family responsibilities, health, life in general, why make things even harder for yourself?

It's like that saying when you owe the bank a million, they own you. When you owe the bank a billion, you own them. Three years later I watched another company Thestreet.com only took 10% of almost disappear because Thestreet.com was not obligated to follow through.

So, at that point, without even having a site finished (**or even started**): I knew I had three things going for me:

A)   I was going to get traffic. I could write three or four articles a day and link each one back to Stockpickr all over the article. The street.com got 100mm page-views a month so I knew I would get some percentage of that.

B)   I was going to make money. If I got even 3 million page-views a month and the average CPM of Thestreet.com (according to their SEC filings) was $17, I would make about $50 thousand a month with expenses nearing zero. What if I put 3 ads a page on the site? Then I would make even more. Slap a 40x multiple on a growing company and before I even started I had real value.

C)   Profitability and growth from day one meant I could put the company up for sale almost immediately. But that's another story.

With my first successful company, Reset, I had about 10 paying customers before I finally made the jump to running the company fulltime: HBO, Interscope, BMG, New Line Cinema, and Warner Brothers were all paying customers before I jumped ship from HBO to run Reset fulltime.

When I started my fund of hedge funds I didn't put one dime into the expense of setting it up until I had the first $20 million commitment. $20 million with a 1.5% management fee meant an instant $300 thousand in revenues, plus extra money for legal fees, etc. Enough to pay a salary or two. It took a year of cultivating my network before I had that commitment, but it worked.

This is just me, personally. Some people don't mind starting a company without any customers. I'm too conservative for this. I'm happy to even give up equity to get that first customer. 50% of a profitable company is better than 100% of a company that will probably quickly go out of business.

How do you get that first customer?

-       **Who**? List the 20 CEOs or high level executives you would like to meet. If you have a rolodex, great. If you don't, then you might have to write to 40 people. This is why it's important to Exploit your Employer (see the post with this title at jamesaltucher.com) and use some of the other ideas mentioned throughout this book. But it's OK if your rolodex is cold. Many successful businesses I've been involved with started with cold emails.

-       **Ideas**. Develop 20 ideas for each person. Get your idea muscle in shape first. [See chapter on How to be the Luckiest Person Alive].

-       **Communicate**. Write them all, giving at least 10 of the ideas, in detail, and how you would implement them. Sometimes you have to dig for their email address. [See post on jamesaltucher.com on how I chased down Stevie Cohen].

-       **Meet**. All this does is getting you the meeting. Once you're in the door, the conversation can go anywhere. Of the 20 people you write, rule of the universe is you'll get six meetings.

-       **Ask**. In the meetings ask the question: "**What one product can I build for you that you will definitely buy?**" Remember, execution is a commodity. Because of globalization you can build anything for cheap. I built the first working version of Stockpickr.com for $3000 in Bangalore. Throw in another $150 from a design made in Siberia. You need zero skillset for that. Just a good idea muscle, an ability to sell, and modest ability to manage a project.

-       **Never say No**. Never. If someone says, "can you do this?" Yes. "But can you do this?" Yes. Can you do it for this? Yes.

-       **Follow up every day**. Nice to meet you. Here's my sketch of what you want. Is this right? Should I start today?

-       **Equity**. If necessary, give up equity for that first customer. Or the first two customers.

-       **Done**. If more than one CEO wants the same product or service, and the price is right, then now you have a business. Build the product, sell it and you're in shape.

-       **Repeat**. You're not really "Done". Every day you have to go back and see if your customer is achieving more success BECAUSE of your products. If he is, then ask him what else he needs and then build it. If he isn't, then ask him what else he needs and builds it. Your easiest new sales will be with your old customers.

This has worked for me on three different occasions. And each time resulted in great profit's for me. By the way, this technique has also worked for people who have contacted me with their own ideas.

Listen. You've been hypnotized. You've been told you need a corporate job. You need a college degree. You need stability. You need the white picket fence. You need the IRA and the health insurance. Snap your fingers in front of your face. The American Religion is a myth, just like the movie, Thor, is based on a myth. Stability is only in your mind. There's $15 trillion dollars in our economy, recession or no recession. It's falling like snow. Reach out with your tongue and taste it.

CHAPTER NINE
How to Live Forever

Let's say you knew that on December 15, 2020, you were going to die in Springfield, Illinois. What would you do? Well, for starters you would probably prolong your life simply by avoiding Springfield, Illinois on December 15, 2020. It just so happens we can use statistics to see the future, and by doing so, can postpone death as long as possible.

I'm sick of the anti-aging industry. Basically, nothing fancy works. Dr. Oz recommends reservatrol but scientific studies only show that enormous amounts of it are what extends the lifespan of a mouse. There's no way to take an equivalent amount as a human. Anti-aging expert Andrew Weil often suggests herbal remedies instead of pharmaceutical medicines but I think, again, the research is very unclear and it's no secret that lifespans have gone up in general with the rise of more readily available, FDA-approved pharmaceuticals. There's always a lot of discussion of homeopathic medicine but, again, the evidence is lacking.

My view is to take a very common sense view towards aging. By the way, I have never thought about anti-aging techniques before. But I'm 42-years-old now, and probably past the half-point of my life, so I've started to wonder about it. Common sense has served me well in most other areas of my life. Hippocrates, the father of modern medicine, puts it succinctly with "Do no harm" in his Hippocratic oath. There's a similar rule in the area of financial advice which I think applies here as well. It's actually two rules, stated by Warren Buffett, the greatest investor ever: "Rule No. 1: Don't Lose Money. Rule No. 2: Don't Forget Rule #1."

The Warren Buffett approach is appealing. Think about it from a financial perspective. Most of the reasons people go broke is not because they failed to make money but because they spent their hard-earned money on bad investments that went to zero. In other words, they broke Buffett's rules. Much more important than figuring out how to add dollars to your net worth is how to avoid losing the dollars you've already accumulated. Applied to the anti-aging industry — don't spend so much time figuring out how to add years to your lifespan. How about use common sense to make sure you don't make additional decisions that cost you your health.

We know what the main killers are in life (this comes from the Centers for Disease Control, U.S. Government, data):

Top 10 Killers

Heart disease: 616,067

Cancer: 562,875

Stroke (cerebrovascular diseases): 135,952

Chronic lower respiratory diseases: 127,924

Accidents (unintentional injuries): 123,706

Alzheimer's disease: 74,632

Diabetes: 71,382

Influenza and Pneumonia: 52,717

Nephritis, nephrotic syndrome, and nephrosis: 46,448

Septicemia: 34,828

So let's start by avoiding some of these diseases.

1. **No Smoking**. You only have to go to the American Heart Organization website to see their research on how smoking is related to heart disease. A quote: "Smoking increases blood pressure, decreases exercise tolerance and increases the tendency for blood to clot. Smoking also increases the risk of recurrent coronary heart disease after bypass surgery." That doesn't sound good. There are also numerous studies on the effects of smoking on cancer. Go to cancer.gov. Here's a quote: "Of the 250 known harmful chemicals in tobacco smoke, more than 50 have been found to cause cancer. These chemicals include:

>
> arsenic (a heavy metal toxin)
>
> benzene (a chemical found in gasoline)
>
> beryllium (a toxic metal)
>
> cadmium (a metal used in batteries)
>
> chromium (a metallic element)
>
> ethylene oxide (a chemical used to sterilize medical devices)
>
> nickel (a metallic element)
>
> polonium-210 (a chemical element that gives off radiation)
>
> vinyl chloride (a toxic substance used in plastics manufacture)

That's pretty bad. I just have to read the first: "arsenic." Who wants to put arsenic in their body? Don't forget rule #1!

2. **No Heavy Drinking**. Note that I say "heavy" drinking and not drinking in general. In fact, many studies show that moderate drinking reduces the risk of heart attacks by up to 40 percent. Go to this link: http://www2.potsdam.edu/hansondj/HealthIssues/1109728 149.html .

It has a list of studies that show the types of cancers that moderate drinking actually help prevent. What is moderate versus heavy drinking? At cdc.goc, "drinking in moderation is defined as having no more than one drink per day for women and no more than two drinks per day for men."

Heavy drinking, on the other hand, is lethal. Obviously, it increases your risk of having a fatal accident, but there's numerous studies showing that heavy drinking is linked to various cancers, heart disease, and Alzheimer's. Here's a quote from Alzinfo.org: "In the study, researchers found that the combination of heavy drinking and heavy smoking sped up the age of onset of Alzheimer's by six to seven years. That is a considerable number, making them among the most important preventable risk factors for Alzheimer's disease." Oh yeah, there's that smoking thing again.

On heartdisease.about.com: "After their heart attacks, patients who had done any binge drinking during the previous year had a death rate that was 73 percent higher than patients who did not do any binge drinking. Even occasional binge drinking (as they defined that term in this study) increased the risk of death." Binge drinking they define as having three or more beers in a day.

From the American Cancer Society: "Death from liver cancer is higher among heavy alcohol users than among people who do not drink."

So it's pretty simple. You can avoid accidents, heart disease and a bunch of cancers if you never drink more than two beers a day.

3. **Sex**. It doesn't have to be all puritan. Maybe you like to smoke and drink a lot and now you're pretty upset. How about taking up a more fun activity during the day, like sex. Here's an article by Jonah Lehrer: "Sex is stressful but good for you."

See it here: (http://www.wired.com/wiredscience/2010/08/sex-is-stressful-but-good-for-you/)

Basically it shows that sex activates various hormones that increases your immune system, decreases your stress levels, reduces the risk of Alzheimer's, and all sorts of other good things. And it's pretty much common sense that this is a good thing. Heck, the Bible recommends we do a lot of it.

There's an article from WebMd on the 10 health benefits of sex. (http://www.webmd.com/sex-relationships/features/10-surprising-health-benefits-of-sex?page=2) One quote: "The researchers also found that having sex twice or more a week reduced the risk of fatal heart attack by half for the men, compared with those who had sex less than once a month."

4. **No snacking**. Obesity is linked to high blood pressure, heart disease, diabetes, certain types of cancer, etc. There's no shame in being obese. Over one-third of adult Americans are obese according to the Centers for Disease Control. And being overweight and enjoying food are not crimes. But if you stick to the basics you'll avoid (reduce) being obese. Ugh, I'm really hungry right this second as I'm writing this. Since last year whenever the market's gone down I've felt an irresistible urge to eat. I'll eat an

apricot Danish, or a corn muffin, or a hot dog, Pringles, Doritos, or anything with Cajun spices. If you have some corned beef hash when I'm in this state, please send it over. I'll eat all of it. I'm like a shovel working on Obama's trillion dollars' worth of road repairs, I'll shove it all in.

This is not a healthy lifestyle and now that I'm about to breach the age of 42 I have to think about my metabolism and how it's beginning to weaken. This happened to me once before, towards the tail end of the bear market of 2002. My entire life I've weighed my college weight except for that one time in 2002 when I gained about 20 lbs. I read through all the diet books and nutrition sites but none of them made sense to me. So I came up with my own diet and it worked. What follows is the "James Altucher White Book Diet" as seen on Oprah, The View, the Today Show, Obama's Inaugural speech, and other top Nielsen rated TV shows [note from ed. Unable to verify] . It took me about two months to lose the 20 pounds once I started using this plan

No sodas. Ever. One can of coke contains 16 sugars. That's just mindless calories.

No snacks between meals. Have a breakfast, lunch, and dinner. And that's it.

No white at night. Meaning, no pasta, no ice cream, no cheese, no bread. Nothing white at night. Enjoy a steak and some asparagus.

One item for breakfast. Knock yourself out if you want a croissant. Or a bagel with cream cheese. Or a fruit cup. Or one Belgian waffle. But stick to only one item.

Do whatever you want for lunch. Doesn't matter as long as you stick to the other rules above. And if you are also avoiding the heavy drinking then your calories will stay down and your weight might go down.

5. **Exercise**. I know, everyone says this. I don't want to be boring so we'll keep this simple and stick to the minimal basics. First off, it's obvious that exercise and being in shape has health benefits. From the Mayo Clinic, there's an article on the benefits of exercise. (http://www.mayoclinic.com/health/exercise/HQ01676) A quote: "Regular physical activity can help you prevent — or manage — high blood pressure. Your cholesterol will benefit, too. Regular physical activity boosts high-density lipoprotein (HDL), or good cholesterol while decreasing triglycerides. This one-two punch keeps your blood flowing smoothly by lowering the buildup of plaques in your arteries."

And there's more. "Regular physical activity can help you prevent type-2 diabetes, osteoporosis and certain types of cancer."

BAM! We avoid the two top killers and probably a bunch more.

If you are already an exercise fanatic, then this section isn't for you. But if you are not really that into exercise or you get bored with it then we need to figure out how to trick your mind and body into getting motivated to exercise. Minimally, you want to do a half hour of exercise a day but that can be spread out. Some ideas:

Can you wake up 10 minutes earlier and do 30 push-ups and 30 sit-ups? If all you did was 100 push-ups a day, spread out throughout the day (do 30 more during a commercial break, for instance), you're going to get in good shape and build muscle.

Can you take the stairs instead of an escalator whenever you get the chance?

Can you park a little further from work and walk a half mile instead of parking right at the door?

Take a tango lesson once a week or ballroom dancing. Or play a couple of games of tennis or even ping pong. Anything that can get you to sweat a little bit.

Find a basketball court and just try to shoot 10 baskets. Just the jumping and shooting is decent exercise for 10 minutes and might be fun.

Get someone to show you two to four yoga poses. Do them every day.

The key is just to get the body moving in a way that's new and a little more difficult than its usual movements (sitting down, sleeping and eating). And if you're really motivated and just want to get through a half hour of solid exercise, just do 100 push-ups, 100 sit ups, and 100 squats in a half hour period. Do it three times a week and you're set for life.

7. **Sleep a lot**. Sleeping is great. For one thing, when you sleep, you probably won't have a fatal accident. Nor will you be eating while you sleep, or drinking heavily or smoking, or any of the other activities that can cause an inconveniently timed death. In fact, lack of sleep (meaning six hours or less on average) is linked to colon cancer, weight gain, strokes, heart disease, high blood pressure,

high cholesterol, depression. Don't we all like to sleep a little more? Certainly sleeping an extra hour a day has got to be a lot easier than exercising an hour a day.

So how much sleep do you need? Seven to eight hours a night. More than that is not even necessarily healthy. Statistics show that people who regularly sleep eight hours a night, no more and no less, live the longest.

I have insomnia. I've also been day trading for a living, on and off, for the past ten years. I've traded my own money and others. It's an unpleasant way to live. The highs are very high and the lows are very low and painful. Whether you are at the highs or the lows you're probably going to experience insomnia along with 32 million other people in this country that have insomnia.

When I have insomnia here is the form it takes: I have no problem falling asleep. But then at about 2 or 3am, I am awake and can't get back to sleep. The worst is when I finally get back to sleep around 5:30 but by then I'm in trouble: I'll wake up around 6:30 or 7 completely exhausted for the day.

Some of the suggestions below may seem harsh. And the correct solution for insomnia will be different for everyone. But if you do follow the suggestions below, I can safely say it's unlikely you will have insomnia.

> - No computer for the last hour of the day. Not only that, turn off the computer. There should be no computer sound or monitor light. The sound and light keeps you sucked into the virtual reality of the day trading world, where you live and die on every tick in the markets. You need to

disengage from that world and enter back into the real world in order to sleep.

- No food after 7pm. I really meant to write 5pm but that might be unrealistic for most people. Sleep and digestion are closely linked. Studies show that many people with insomnia have either irritable bowel syndrome (IBS) or sensitive stomachs. Not eating past 5pm and drinking more liquids throughout the day can help you be cleaned out for your sleep. You want to eat easy-to-digest foods at night. No meat, not too much sugar. Vegetables and fruits.

- No alcohol. The sugar will pop you awake in the middle of the night.

- Exercise. This is directly related to what happens to your body when you day trade. Imagine if you were mugged. Adrenalin and stress hormones would get released in your body and you'd either fight or flight. Fighting or running would work off those stress hormones. When you day trade, it's as if you are getting mugged all day long — but you are just sitting there. You aren't working off the stress hormones. Those chemicals will keep you awake at night. Exercise (if done early in the day) will at first increase the stress hormones but then over the next few hours after exercise finishes, will work those hormones off.

- Clean your bedroom, your closet, your office, your kitchen, etc. Your mind and your living space need to be friends with each other. Clean mind equals clean living space. Cluttered space means cluttered mind. Cluttered mind leads to anxiety, nervousness, stress, and then those stress hormones are waking you up again in the middle of the night. Power down the computer and clean your room before you go to sleep.

- Put closure on the end of your work day. Make a list of the work related things you did that day. Write them down on a pad. Trades you made, articles you read that you remember, ideas you had, calls you made related to business. I write everything into an email I send to myself. It helps me to see how productive I was (or not), particularly on days that might not have been that good otherwise (i.e. if I lost money trading that day). It also helps me understand and analyze my trades a bit more. And finally, when I hit "send" on that email to myself, my day is over. Onwards to the next thing (talking to family, friends, etc.)

- Meditate. You don't need to get in the lotus position and start chanting for an hour or two. Most of the time during the day, particularly when you're stressed, you may stop and notice that your breaths are short and uneven. Sit in a chair for ten minutes, with the lights out or on dim. Simply watch your breath. Don't breathe too deeply but as deeply as is natural. Count the breaths to ten. Then start over. If you find you are losing your place too much (or slipping into "11..12..") then just count to five and start over. Do that for just ten minutes in the evening. Ideally, do it in the morning also before you begin your day.

- Early to bed, early to rise. Ben Franklin is right. This will make you wealthy (maybe wise also but we're focused on trading here). 5am is a good time to wake up, read the news, check futures, and plan your trades for the day. That gives you a little over 4 hours to get ready for the trading day. If you need 8 hours of sleep then backtrack from 5am to see when you need to get to sleep.

If you follow these guidelines you will be on your A game when you trade, you will sleep better, and you will wake up each morning refreshed and ready to go.

7. **Regular Flow**. You know what I mean: constipation is bad. Imagine keeping all that horrible bacteria in your body one more second than you have to. Get it out! What happens is that fecal matter builds up in your colon, causing an un-virtuous cycle: the more fecal matter that builds up, blocking the openings of the colon, the more fecal matter gets stuck up there, putrefying for years, leading to everything from colon cancer to a breakdown of the immune system: more flus, allergies, heart disease, etc. The key to this entire article is how to very simply avoid the leading causes of death. Keeping the inside of your body clean is the simplest. Going to the bathroom more than three times a week is key. Everyone varies in this but ideally, at least once a day is enough to keep the factory working.

How to avoid constipation:

Use it or lose it. When you have to go ... GO!

High fiber diet: fruits, vegetables, high fiber cereals (Dr. John Harvey Kellog, the founder of Kellog's cereal, invented his high-bran, high fiber cereal for just this purpose).

Lots of liquids

Avoid eating too much low-fiber foods. Obviously we all like our ice cream. But too march starch and sugar could be bad, particularly if you are currently suffering.

8. **Feel Gratitude**. Stress affects every aspect of your physical health and can cause every single one of the causes of death mentioned above. Every technique described above indirectly reduces stress. But dealing with stress also involves building your mental muscles. Mental muscles are like physical ones — they atrophy. If you are bedridden for a few months then you would have to engage in intense physical rehab in order to even walk because your muscles would've atrophied that severely and quickly.

It's the same with mental muscles. The muscle that prevents stress needs to be regularly exercised or you will succumb to the excesses of too much stress in your life and you won't be able to climb out of the hole. Believe me, I know this. At different times in my life I've made and lost millions. Part of what I do is I day trade for a living. While there are many stressful jobs out there, day trading has to be among the top 10. When I'm in a big position and it starts moving against me I feel every heartbeat in my body pushing the blood all around. The stress permeates me and part of the daily routine of a day trader is learning to deal with the stress.

Think of the human body when its mugged, or when a car is bearing down on it. The human body signals a flight or fight response. Your adrenalin pumps through and its almost as if you have superhuman powers as you either run the fastest you've ever run, or you jump out of the way of a car or, god hoping, you block a car from running over your baby, as has happened in extreme examples. In other words, in a normal response to stress you feel the stress, your body produces the adrenalin and hormones to deal with it, and you react, quickly working off the stress.

But the normal daily grind that causes our stress almost never gets worked off. It's as if you are mugged all day long. And that leads to only bad things in the body.

There are many ways to avoid stress but the one I'm focusing on in this technique is to exercise your gratitude muscle. Try it for just five minutes a day. List all of the things you are grateful for. Don't think about anything else. You don't need to meditate with the Dalai lama to reduce stress. All you have to do is for five minutes a day think about the things you are grateful for. Your kids. Your friends. The walk you took yesterday. The smile a stranger through your way this morning.

Once the muscle is exercised, get it working again during the moments you feel stressed. If you are feeling stress about a family relationship, think about a time when that relationship was great in your life. If you are feeling stressed about money, remember that all things cycle and whatever you have this second is still enough for you to enjoy life. I know it sounds corny. But if you do that five minutes a day I can guarantee that you'll be surprised at the new muscles you find.

9. **Mental exercises**. Nobody knows for sure how every detail of the brain works. But we do have a basic model. The brain has 100mm neurons, give or take, that communicate via synapses. When you learn something new, a bunch of neurons and their synapses fire up with traffic. The more traffic between neurons, the more their synapses strengthen. Like in the Gratitude section above, if we keep on strengthening the synapses between neurons all across the brain then we build up resistance to any illnesses that effect the brain, such as Alzheimer's, the #6 killer above. Additionally, there are other benefits to keeping sharp: higher income, perhaps less stress, hopefully an ability to avoid accidents (like balancing your checkbook incorrectly), etc.

Some mental exercises you can do daily to keep sharp:

Play memory games. Exercise your memory

Get a book of brain teasers and puzzles and solve them.

Play chess, checkers, poker, any game that requires some strategic thought and memorization.

After meeting a person, try to remember everything he or she wore and said.

Try to eat lefty every once in a while (or right-handed if you are left-handed).

Right now try to figure out what coins are in your pocket just by touch. Now do the same for bills (100 dollar bills are less worn than ones)

Play boggle or any other game which takes a set of letters and you try to see how many new words you can form from it.

Like physical exercise, if you do mental exercises for 20-30 minutes a day for five days a week you'll see dramatic results in a very short time.

10. **Avoid hospitals**. Something like 40,000 people die each year from infections they get in the hospital according the CDC. Essentially, hospitals are filled with bacteria and hospital staff (not in every hospital, but some) routinely ignores the basic steps required to insure that people do not pass infections to others.

Make sure anyone who touches you washes their hands first.

Don't read the magazines (or, if you are a kid, play with the toys) in the waiting lounges at hospitals or doctor's rooms.

Have an advocate with you preferably at all times.

A quick story: I was once pretending to be a respiratory therapist for a week in a hospital (long story) and I got to walk around with doctors, other respiratory therapists, etc. on their routines. It wasn't uncommon to hear a story such as "such and such nurse took the tracheotomy tube out but forgot to plug it up and the patient suffocated." Again, not every hospital is like this but mistakes are made. There are millions of surgical procedures a year. Some complicated and some simple and all it takes is a tiny percentage of those to go wrong and the number of deaths from surgery accidents will far exceed the number of deaths from plane crashes each year. "The number of adverse events each year (is) equivalent to 13 jumbo jets crashing and killing all 350 passengers on board," Kevin Rudd's Australian National Health and Hospital Reform Commission says. An advocate every step of the way can insure that proper procedures are being followed.

Question all surgeries. If the doctor says "can you do surgery next Tuesday," find out first if there's any other non-surgical procedures. I hate to be blasphemous to the medical industry but first check with an acupuncturist (a good one that is recommended by friends who were actually helped by that acupuncturist) or a chiropractor. See if physical rehab can help first, or at least be tried without detrimental effects to the body part in question.

If you must do surgery make sure the surgeon has ample experience (no students!) and make sure a checklist is used during the procedure (Atul Gawande has an excellent book on the topic of doctors using checklists.)

You want to get out of the hospital as quickly as possible if you are having surgery there. Here's a basic tip: Don't have your surgery on a Thursday. Doctors don't want to work on a weekend. You might be stuck there for the whole weekend if you just need to be in the hospital for a max two days.

If you are using a teaching hospital, try to avoid going there (if possible) during July. There is the notorious "July Effect" when interns become residents; residents become full-time doctors, etc. It's the first time many of these new doctors are full time in their specialty and may not have the experience yet to accurately diagnose and prescribe the right medicines, etc. Here's an article on the dangers of July in a hospital. (http://idiopathicmedicine.wordpress.com/2010/06/30/the-dangers-of-july-in-the-hospital/)

Make sure the doctor has clear handwriting on prescriptions. Believe it or not, the famous ability of pharmacists to read the handwriting of doctors is just not true. Here's a recent article (http://www.time.com/time/health/article/0,8599,1578074,00.html) claiming that 7,000 deaths per year are caused by poor handwriting on prescriptions.

Avoid being plugged into an IV. If you can swallow liquids, drink the water, don't have it put into you via a possibly contaminated IV unit.

11. **Cleanliness**. This one is obvious. We collect bacteria throughout the day by touching doorknobs, staircase rails, elevator buttons, shaking hands, eating food, etc. Also, there's the saying: "clean desk, clean mind." In other words, keeping our environment clean is not only physically healthy but helps to reduce stress and makes you more productive. Reducing stress, as mentioned above, is key to avoiding many of the diseases that cause death.

Wash hands every time you go from outside to inside. Under the nails is one of the dirtiest parts of the entire body and once you take those nails and rub your eyes or scratch an itch, you are infecting yourself with any bacteria that grabbed onto the inside of those nails. Keep them short. Wash them regularly.

Brush your teeth. Bacteria is all over your mouth. Brushing after every meal is keep and before you go to sleep and after you wake up. It sounds annoying but brushing, flossing, and using a tongue scraper for anything that stays attached to your tongue will help prevent any disease and, of course, keep your breath clean.

Make your bed. Who doesn't like to come home to a made bed.

This is a drag but shower every morning and night. When you go to sleep at night you have a whole day's worth of bacteria on you. Why take that bacteria and put it all over your nice clean sheets when you can avoid it?

12. **Avoid accidents**. This almost seems like an oxymoron. The word "accident" implies there is some degree of luck involved. Like you were walking along outside of a building and something falls out of a high up window and hits you. That's an accident that seems like just bad luck. Or is it? We know that 123,000 accidents a year occur. So let's break that down a little further.

About half the accidental deaths come from car accidents. So one thing we can do is simply avoid getting in cars. Now, that's not always possible because we need cars to get to work. But a couple of thoughts:

> - If you have a choice: live closer to work. Or take public transportation.

> - If you don't have a choice: try to avoid doing more than one activity at a time while in the car.

Don't eat, talk on the cell phone, don't play with the radio.

- Don't jaywalk (don't be the recipient of a car accident if it's easy to avoid).

- Wear a seat belt

- About 1/3 of accidents happen at home. Don't get fancy and try to fix the TV antenna on the roof. Don't get on a ladder if you don't have to. Be careful when walking down stairs, etc.

The anti-aging industry makes billions trying to get you to take fancy pills, buy expensive equipment, do expensive medical tests, etc. But sometimes the simplest way to live longer is to avoid all the ways you were going to die.

CHAPTER TEN

When there is a Mouse in the Salad then You Are Growing Too Fast

A few months ago I was playing backgammon with Stephen Dubner when we saw something that was fairly repulsive. Here's the thing about Dubner. He wrote Freakonomics and that catapulted him to success. And I think it's a great book. But here's the thing: I think he's a world-class writer with his other books. "Confessions of a Hero Worshipper" is one of my all-time favorites but I don't think it sold well.

Stephen writes in his first book, "Turbulent Souls" that his dad died when he was young. In "Confessions" he admits to worshipping the football player Franco Harris from the Pittsburgh Steelers. Stephen and I are near the same age and I liked football as a kid so I remember who Harris was. He was a machine for the Steelers. Anyway, Stephen wants to write about the concept of hero worship. He has various philosophical ideas about what hero worship means in our society. How it could be a replacement for fatherhood. It could even be a replacement for God (he notes that the authors of almost every major superhero (Superman, etc., were Jewish) and even Superman's real name "Kal-El" is derived from the Hebrew word for "God" - "El".

But he doesn't just write about these things. He goes ahead and does them. He went to Pittsburgh, called Franco Harris, and waited for Franco Harris to basically call him back. Harris did! And for the next few months Dubner went back and forth between hanging out with Harris or waiting for Harris to call him back. Harris was a childhood hero come to life. Maybe they could be friends? Stephen gave it his all. And the book morphs from this philosophical tome about heroes and fathers and gods to Stephen's unrequited friendship with Franco Harris, the 70s Pittsburgh Steelers all-pro football player.

I hope Stephen eventually writes more books like that. I might've even been telling him this while we were eating at Le Pain Quotidien on the upper west side and playing backgammon. He might have even been beating me in that particular moment so the interruption was welcome. The woman at the table next to us started in with a combination of screaming and crying. It's one of those animal sounds when all the animals around sense something is very wrong and look over. Here's what was wrong:

There was a dead mouse in her salad. She moved it from the salad to a bowl. I walked over there and asked her if I could take a picture so she could have it in case she needed it for anything. I was being nice and she thanked me profusely but my real motive is exactly what you are seeing here: I wanted to write about it.

Le Pain Quotidien is a great chain of healthy restaurants. But it's growing fast. When a company grows fast things (mice) literally slip through the cracks. Stephen did a radio show about the situation a few weeks ago. I said on the show, a lot of things have to go wrong in order for that mouse to get there. It's not a simple mistake. A bag of salad had to be left open in a kitchen, unobserved. A mouse had to crawl into it. The salad bag had to be then shut. The mouse then died. At some point in the future the salad was removed from storage and opened. A hand reached into the bag and didn't watch what it was doing. It pulled out a bunch of lettuce, and one dead mouse, and put it on a woman's plate. All unnoticed.

Things happen from the top down. It's not the waiter's fault. Or the guy in the kitchen's fault. Or the manager's. Somewhere near the top of a fast growing company, an executive can't handle the growth, and doesn't put the structure in place for a mouse to sneak into the salad bag. This happens with every company on the planet. A mouse in the salad means congrats, you are growing. But it also means if you can't handle the growth, you're about to die a horrible death. Trapped without oxygen in a salad bag.

A waiter had to then take the plate, and still not notice the dead mouse that was on it. It was delivered to the woman. The woman began eating the salad. Until she ate enough lettuce to uncover the mouse, or until she stuck her fork in it and picked it up.

Stephen put on his Freakonomics hat. We didn't pay our bill and we packed up our backgammon set and began walking out. "Let's let the manager set the price of the bill for us." At the door, the manager came up to us. Stephen said: "look, we mostly finished our meal but now we don't feel so well, given the mouse thing. What do you suggest we pay for this meal?"

Stephen's theory was that if the manager was good, he would have us pay nothing, even offer us incentives to come back. Fortunately it turns out the manager was good.

As we were leaving, the woman who found the mouse in her salad came up to me and said, "thank you so much. You are very kind to help me out here." No problem, I said, I wanted to help. I would hate to find a mouse in my food. I was actually feeling a gag reflex as I was thinking about it. I think I'm feeling that even right now as I write this.

She was still thanking me. "It's very sweet that you would help us. My friend and I eat here regularly. Maybe we will see you when we eat here next week."

What?

CHAPTER ELEVEN
You Can Call Yourself An Entrepreneur When...

It's not really such a great thing to be an entrepreneur. There's no real "freedom" in it. People think that starting your own business gives you freedom. It doesn't. When you work a corporate job where you only, realistically, work for 1-2 hours a day and you can leave your work at the office, then you have freedom.

Entrepreneurship == slavery. You are a slave to employees, partners, investors, a board, clients, potential buyers, reporters, landlords, random people off the street who try to come into your office and rob you, etc.

On Quora recently someone asked "When can I call myself an entrepreneur". I'm happy to share some general guidelines:

If someone hasn't had this experience, they shouldn't call themselves an entrepreneur:

Lying awake at 3 in the morning wondering about:

A) I think I have to kiss a lot of ass tomorrow. Note to self: bring up with therapist that I never really feel like "the real me" anymore.

B) How am I going to make payroll next week

C) how do I solve the fact that Wade (employee #6) now has a bad attitude that is spreading to the others (i.e. they smoke cigarettes in stairwell discussing reasons they hate me. I know this because I tape-recorded it).

D) How do I deal with the complaints from client #1 about employee #3?

E) How quickly can I package this company up to sell the damn thing so I can sleep again?

F) The site is too slow. How can I find a programmer who knows what he's doing?

G) I have 8 new features in my head. Can I get them up on the site within 24 hours?

H) I missed the insurance payment. I hope to god none of my employees get hit by a car this month.

I) Why won't Client #2 pay his bills on time? Should I hire someone to break his legs?

J) Is it me? Do I need to improve my sales technique? Do I need to donate to someone's charity again?

K) Why do I feel every pulse of my blood running through my whole body right now?

L) Is it 6am yet? Oh shoot, it's only 3:05am. I've been thinking about all this stuff for only 5 minutes. Should I get up and work or try to sleep. I'll try to sleep. I'll count sheep. But only after I figure out how to make payroll.

M) My competitors are all better than me. And they all go to parties where they meet clients and make money.

N) Can I introduce my potential client to a potential girlfriend?

O) How come we didn't get enough publicity for our launch? Is it because I'm not cool enough?

Oh, and if you have never used these phrases you shouldn't call yourself an entrepreneur:

- "I don't like to say anything bad about my competitors. They are all good guys and I respect their work. After all, this is a big enough field that we've all become friends. But perhaps the one difference we have with them is..." (to potential client)

- "The pay is not a lot right now but this is only temporary while we look at putting you into more of a management position." (to potential employee)

- "This particular job is not fun but we have some fun stuff coming up that we can put you on." (to potential employee again. He is about to get screwed).

- "I can get that done by end of the week, no problem" (thinking: by end of month or two, no problem)

- "of course you have insurance" (to employee. Please don't get sick that week)

- "We have plans to open offices in various parts of the world" (to potential buyer, in front of map with pins in China, Paris, London, NYC, LA).

- "Just come inside and sit at a desk" (to random people walking in street right before potential buyer of company visits). I'm not kidding.

- "We want to work with you. Just tell us what you can pay and we'll be happy." (to get client to say 'yes' before you start telling him about add-ons)

- "Of course it's legal"

- (to secretary when taking prospective client out to lunch, in front of prospective client) "HOLD ALL CALLS. I don't want to be bothered at all for the next two to four hours. This is a very important lunch!"

- "We can do that" (to anyone who asks you about anything)

- "I'm going to be personally involved in this project." (Me, to anyone)

- "your sales should triple after this" (to client who hires us)

- "I agree with you completely. I'm going to improve that." (to client who tells you why he doesn't like you)

- "Chances are electricity in NYC will keep running on Jan 1, 2000 if you hire us" (I said to Con Ed, when hiring us for a Y2K project)

Oh, and you cannot call yourself an entrepreneur until:

- You've logged at least 60,000+ useless air miles (in a 3 month period)

- You cry with hands over your head thinking, 'what the hell did I just do' (remind me to tell you about the time I met Tupac's mom)

- You get a crush on at least one employee

- You've gotten a 4 page email from an ex-employee listing all of the reasons they don't like you anymore (now friends with that ex-employee)

-    You realize you've suddenly been defriended on Facebook by a reasonable chunk of ex-employees)

-    You think of four new businesses you'd rather be starting than this stupid one.

Howard Lindzon called me while I was writing this to see how I liked the new blog design his guys did for me. I figured I'd add to the blog-post on jamesaltucher.com: 53 things I've learned from Howard Lindzon so I asked him, "Howard, how do you know when you can call yourself an entrepreneur?"

I was sort of disappointed in his answer:

"You can call yourself an entrepreneur when you wake up at 3am and you are super excited to get to the office and begin the day."

CHAPTER TWELVE
How to Steal and Get Rich

My eight year old daughter is crying right now. She's trying to draw manga-style comic book figures. "The eyes look stupid!" she says, "and the arms look flimsy!" My oldest tries to calm her down, "Mollie, I'm three years older than you. That's why my characters look so good," she says, but somehow that doesn't work and it doesn't help when my oldest says, "Mollie, guess what, I finished drawing on the whole pad? Aren't these pretty?"

I tell my youngest: "Mollie, look on the Internet and see how other artists do their eyes and arms. I bet there are some Manga artists who even have videos on how to do it."

She says, "but that's copying. I don't want to copy. I refuse."

So I tell her my favorite quote from Picasso, "Good artists copy. Great artists steal." And my oldest says, "that would mean HE stole." And I tell her that's right but still my youngest refuses to listen. She says, "I don't want to copy. I want to do something completely original." But that's impossible. Just about every idea worked on now is a result of the following recursive formula:

$$NI(X) = NI(1) + NI(2) + NI(3)\ldots + MI$$

Where "NI" = "new idea" and NI1, NI2, etc. equals various new ideas as of yesterday. And "MI" which could be a tiny component of the whole equation, is "My improvement". Which, again, might be minimal, or zero, at best.

Examples:

- **Telescope**. Galileo stole the telescope. He took the original invention by Hans Lippershey, made it a bit longer and more powerful and gets full credit 400 years later for the invention.

- **Telephone**. Who invented the telephone? Well, Alexander Graham Bell of course? But only after the looked at the failed patent Antonio Meucci filed in 1874 (Meucci was too poor to send in the $10 patent charge. So…patent denied. Enter Bell).

- **Relativity**. Einstein stole part of the theory of relativity from Poincare. Poincare published countless papers on relativity that Einstein had studied before his own first book on relativity. Einstein cited hundreds of sources but didn't mention Poincare once. Do the research but there are several instances of direct plagiarism in his initial book on relativity.

- **Search**. Google. Not quite a "steal" in the sense of the above but the entire concept of a "search engine" was dead and over by the time Google hit the scene. My little story on this: A company called "Oingo" came calling one of my partners one day in 2000 or 2001. I forget which year, that's how little impact it made on me. They were working on some algorithm for matching ads with web pages on search engines, or something like that. They needed funding badly. We almost could've named our price. I said, because I was the resident genius, "No way. Isn't the entire search engine business dead?" Somehow they survived, changed their name to Applied Semantics and were bought by a tiny search engine company with no revenues called Google. The Oingo algorithm became "Adsense" which accounts for 99% of Google's revenues. The Applied Semantics deal would've been worth about $1bb - $2bb by now. Suffice to say, Google built on the backs of everyone from Lycos to Oingo to Altavista, etc.

- **Superman**. "Captain Marvel", which was first put out by Fawcett Comics in 1940 was of course a direct rip-off of "Superman" and yet became very successful.

And Superman himself may have been a plagiarism of sorts. 5 years before the first "Superman" came out, Jerry Siegel (Superman's creator) reviewed the book "Gladiator" about a boy growing up in rural America who had super powers.

Siegel claimed in 1940 that Gladiator had not been an inspiration. He did not at that point note his 1932 review of the book.

- **Declaration of Independence**. Thomas Jefferson directly plagiarized John Locke when he wrote the Declaration of Independence. James Madison even admitted later: "The object was to assert, not to discover truths."

- **Chess**. Bobby Fischer learned Russian when he was 14 years old so he could steal ideas from the Russian chess players in the magazine "64". He used those opening ideas to win the US Championship at the age of 15 in the mid-1950s.

- **Art**. Roy Lichtenstein directly stole from the cartoon strip "True Romance" to repackage and then resell for (now) millions.

- **Star Wars**. Whether you call it inspiration or plagiarism, George Lucas took ideas from everything from Taoism to Asimov's Foundation series, to Joseph Campbell, Greek Mythology, King Arthur, etc.

- **Lady Gaga**. She has taken elements from Madonna, to Elton John, to Queen.

-    **Vonnegut**. Kurt Vonnegut said he "cheerfully ripped off" the plot of Brave New World for his novel, "Player Piano"- and Aldous Huxley, in turn, stole it from Eugene Zamatian's "We"

-    **Groupon** and every other business. Almost all current successful internet businesses are the result of lifting (and improving) the ideas from past businesses. Groupon is a direct descendant of the failed Paul Allen company, Mercata (remember?). Facebook (remember Geocities? Or, heaven forbid, Tripod). And why didn't the "World Wide Web Worm:" succeed (the first search engine that I can think of).

-    **Comedy**. In standup comedy, stealing (or improving on) routines has been common. Robin Williams was constantly accused of this early in his career and his reply was that he was so stream of consciousness he sometimes had no idea where the ideas were coming from (i.e., they were coming from his friends even minutes after their acts). Bill Cosby has admitted stealing some jokes from George Carlin, Rosie O'Donnell was known to borrow from Jerry Seinfeld early in their careers. Sam Kinison has accused Bill Hicks of joke thievery who, in turn, has accused Denis Leary of stealing parts of his routine.

-    **3AM**. I personally think Comedy Central's show "Insomnia" is somewhat a rip-off of my III:am idea for HBO (particularly since I pitched the idea to Comedy Central first).

Unfortunately, stealing is not a shortcut to success. **Stealing is THE ONLY PATH to success**.

How do you steal? Try this.

-       **Pick a field you are passionate about**: whether it's blogging,

romance novel writing, comedy, internet entrepreneurship, art, cooking, cancer research, etc.

-       Read everything you can about the field. Here's what you have to read minimally:

•   At least the history of that field from 1800 on. Try to read at least 10 different sources on the history

•   All of the latest blogs in the field. Try to have 100 different sources here.

•   All the basic techniques the current leading experts in the field use. Read all of their biographies or autobiographies.

-       **Pick your five favorite sources in the field**. For instance, if I wanted to write a novel: I'd pick my five favorite novelists. If I wanted to start a business in "local Internet" I'd pick my five favorite local Internet companies. If I wanted to blog, I'd pick my five favorite bloggers. If I wanted to be a management consultant, I'd steal directly from Peter Drucker, Jim Collins, etc.

-       **Get one element that you like from each source**. What element do you think stands out that makes them a success.

-       **Add your own improvement**. Or not. You can even start out with a direct copy and throw in your twist at the end.

-      **Ignore all the haters**. The more people hate you, the more money you will make. Trust me on that.

I'm hoping Mollic grows up and learns how to be just as good a thief as her dad.

CHAPTER THIRTEEN
10 Reasons Why You Should Quit Your Job

Private Equity Firm. I fell straight down and broke both my legs right in the middle of the street. Or strained them. Or something. Because I couldn't walk for a week afterwards. I was walking on Wall Street with two partners in the private equity firm I had just become a partner at earlier that week. This was fairly recently. Like in the past two years. I hadn't stumbled over anything. Just fell to the ground in front of everyone.

"You OK?" everyone asked. I pretended to not limp. Later that night I couldn't walk. A few days later I showed back up at the firm for a meeting I had set up. I wanted to do business with a Brazilian private equity firm. Brazil has two harvests I learned in the meeting. Sounded like a place I wanted to do business. But I got bored. "Excuse me," I said. And I walked out of the meeting. Out of the office. 67 floors down. Subway to Grand Central. Train up the Hudson Valley.

I never went back to the office. "Where are you?" the head partner wrote me. Some phone calls appeared on my cell. "Come back," said the next email. "There's still a place for you here," said the next email two weeks later. I never responded to anything. They might still have my name in the door.

I have some bad habits.

HBO. I couldn't get out of bed in the morning. It was summer. I lived in Hell's Kitchen. For a while, HBO was the best job ever. I used to skip to work every day. But I couldn't get out of bed. And I had a business on the side that was growing. But I was afraid to jump into the abyss and just do my business fulltime. HBO was HBO. I was afraid nobody would return my calls if I left HBO. And I was right. Startup world was the abyss. The work at HBO was monotonous, draining, I hated the politics. I had to go in though. There were meetings. Who was going to make the website for "Sex and the City"?

But I couldn't get out of bed in the morning.

Thestreet.com. I was afraid to go into the office. There were too many people I didn't want to run into. I would do videos outside every morning in front of the New York Stock Exchange. But I refused to go up into the office for meetings. People still stop me on the street, "I used to love those videos. Where are you now?" Even though I write for a million other places. I learned a lot working with Jim Cramer.

But there were too many people I didn't want to run into.

One day, Dave Morrow (R.I.P.) called me and said: "you have to come into the office. We have to talk."

I said: "let's meet outside where you usually do your cigarette breaks." I couldn't come into the office.

"No," he said. "You have to come in."

I had a deal with Thestreet after I sold Stockpickr to them. But two years in, they wanted to change the deal. I went into the office and was met with Dave and the woman from HR. They offered me half salary and I had to show up at the office 40 hours a week.

I'm a skilled negotiator. So I counter-offered. "I will write for you every day for FREE," I said, "and I will get zero salary. But I can't come into the office." At the time I lived on 15 Broad Street. If you know the geography of Wall Street, you would know that I lived approximately 40 feet from Thestreet.com's offices at 14 Wall Street.

They said: "No".

Fund of funds. I ran a fund of hedge funds. We were invested in 12 different hedge funds. This was 2006. Several of those funds have since settled with the SEC. But we were no longer invested in them by then.

A major bank wanted to buy our fund of funds. They made a great offer: 10% of our assets. Typically a company like ours goes for 2% of assets. It was millions. We flew out to California to meet them. They flew out to NYC to meet us. We got the official legal document that was the deal. They wanted me to sign a six year employment agreement. My business partner said we can't do this deal. My lawyer said: "this is indentured servitude."

We didn't respond to the offer. They called me several times. "We are willing to negotiate," the CEO of the bank said, "if there's a problem." But they had no idea what the problem was. Because I never responded to them. I responded to their Facebook friend requests. We're all "friends" now although we've never spoken again. And we shut the fund of funds down.

Trading. I was trading for several hedge funds. But about once a month I would get so stressed I wouldn't be able to sleep and I would feel all the blood going through my body. I'd be up at three in the morning checking futures. I'd never sleep. Once a month my partner and I were convinced we were going to stop trading and make an infomercial for "diet pills".

We figured out how to manufacture them cheap, how to video the infomercial, how to air it late at night. We were going to do it. But we kept trading. And once a month…repeat. We returned the money. Nobody wanted the money back. We were doing great for them. But we returned it all and never spoke to anyone again.

Programming. I had a job at Carnegie Mellon's Center for Machine Translation. Software I wrote helped take Caterpillar tractor manuals and translate them from English to German and ten other languages. One day I left early. I wanted to hang out with a girl. The next day the boss came into my office and, with the door open and in front of people, proceeded to yell at me. But not just yell at me. He was yelling questions. You know those sorts of questions. A yell plus a question you can't answer like, "Did you really think that was a good thing to do?" Of course I can't answer that.

So I quit. And took the job HBO was offering me. But never told him I had a counter-offer. So he would suffer. For months after I left nobody could figure out my programming code. Because I had the ugliest code known to mankind. It was indecipherable.

Xceed. Xceed bought my first company, Reset. They were going to keep all the brands separate but then they combined them and moved us all into one big building. I had an office. I was a "senior vice president" along with about 40 other people. But Xceed had acquired too many companies. Everyone was gossiping all day long about everyone else. I stopped going into the office. I started looking for other things to do. I finally told them I was quitting and they threatened to sue me. "The one area where slavery is legal in America is when one company buys another company," the Chairman of the company told me. So sue me. He has since produced the latest "Superman" movie.

10 Signs you need to leave your corporate job

A)   You can't wake up. You need 10 extra minutes to get up. Then another 10.

B)   You get physically hurt while on the job for no real reason (subconscious at work)

C)   You don't feel like returning emails or phone calls. When the number of unreturned emails or calls hits 20, you need to leave.

D)   You are unsure about your compensation (with the private equity firm above my compensation was very unclear)

E)   You are afraid to run into people in the office for no real reason.

F)   You are not creating any additional value for yourself. View yourself as a business. Is the value of "your business" going up? When I was at the fund of funds, the fact that I could only sell my fund of funds if I signed a six year employment agreement showed me that I had not been creating any additional value in my business.

G)   You are thinking about selling diet pills. Tim Ferris aside, nobody in their right mind should sell diet pills.

H)   Someone yells at you. You're not a kid. Yelling is abusive. Nobody should ever yell at you. Ever. But that's a hard habit to break if you are used to people yelling at you.

I)   You think about office politics more than you think about how to do well at your job. Never gossip at work. Ever.

J)   You date a girl at work. One of you needs to leave. Pronto. Else, work, relationships, life, gets ruined. Don't shit where you eat.

I think 90% of people should quit their jobs right now or do something utterly drastic to shake things up. "What would I do?" people can then ask, "I have responsibilities, mouths to feed, mortgage to pay. You don't get it." Yes I do. You throw yourself into the abyss. You get scared. You stay up late at night thinking and thinking and thinking. You feel like the death of emptiness is worse than the slow death of your job. But you'll figure it out. One by one all of your old colleagues will disappear from your life. They will die.

You'll still be alive

CHAPTER FOURTEEN
Why You Should Never Own a Home
Again

Many people have said to me in the past month, "I'm going to buy a home." Or, "What do you think of the idea of me buying a home?" I like the second batch of people. They are my friends and it seems like they are sincerely asking for my advice. And I'm going to give it to them. Whether they meant it or not.

I have some stories about owning a home. One of them is here: "What It Feels Like to be Rich" where I describe my complete path into utter depravity and insanity. The other one is still too personal. It's filled with about as much pain as I can fit onto a page. Oh, I have a third one also from when I was growing up. But I don't want to upset anyone in my family so I'll leave it out. Oh, I have a fourth story that I just forgot about until this very second. But enough about me. Let's get right to it.

There are many reasons to not buy a home:

A)   **Cash Gone**. You have to write a big fat check for a down payment. "But it's an investment," you might say to me. Historically this isn't true. Housing returned 0.4% per year from 1890 to 2004. And that's just housing prices. It forgets all the other stuff I'm going to mention below. Suffice to say, when you write that check, you're never going to see that money again. Because even when you sell the house later you're just going to take that money and put it into another down payment. So if you buy a $400,000 home, just say goodbye to $100,000 that you worked hard for. You can put a little sign on the front lawn: "$100,000 R.I.P."

B) **Closing costs**. I forget what they were the last two times I bought a house. But it was about another 2-3% out the window. Lawyers, title insurance, moving costs, antidepressant medicine. It adds up. 2-3%.

C) **Maintenance**. No matter what, you're going to fix things. Lots of things. In the lifespan of your house, everything is going to break. Thrice. Get down on your hands and knees and fix it! And then open up your checkbook again. Spend some more money. I rent. My dishwasher doesn't work. I call the landlord and he fixes it. Or I buy a new one and deduct it from my rent. And some guy from Sears comes and installs it. I do nothing. The Sears repairman and my landlord work for me.

D) **Taxes**. There's this myth that you can deduct mortgage payment interest from your taxes. Whatever. That's a microscopic dot on your tax returns. What's worse is the taxes you pay. So your kids can get a great education. Whatever.

E) **You're trapped**. Let's spell out very clearly why the myth of homeownership became religion in the United States. It's because corporations didn't want their employees to have many job choices. So they encouraged them to own homes. So they can't move away and get new jobs. Job salaries is a function of supply and demand. If you can't move, then your supply of jobs is low. You can't argue the reverse, since new adults are always competing with you.

F) **Ugly**. Saying "my house is an investment" forgets the fact that a house has all the qualities of the ugliest type of investment:

Illiquidity. You can't cash out whenever you want.

High leverage. You have to borrow a lot of money in most cases.

No diversification. For most people, a house is by far the largest part of their portfolio and greatly exceeds the 10% of net worth that any other investment should be.

G) **Trapped, part 2**. Some people like to have roots. But I like things to change every once in a while. Starting March, 2009 I was renting an apartment directly across the street from the New York Stock Exchange. It was fun. I'd look out the window and see Wall Street. How exciting! Before that I lived in The Chelsea Hotel with Chubb Rock. Last year we decided to relax and move a little north. Now I look out the window and see the Hudson River. And it's quiet and I can walk along the river in the morning with no noise. It took us two weeks to pick a place and move. No hassles. I like to live a hassle-free life.

H) **Walls**. You can't change the walls when you rent. A lot of people seem to want to tear down walls. Or paint them. Sometimes when you rent you can't do these things. Well, make sure you have a landlord that lets you tear down walls. There must be some ancient evolutionary tic that makes us want to tear down walls or put nails in them or paint them. I don't get it. I like the walls to stay right where they are.

I) **Rent**. People will argue that the price of the mortgage, maintenance taxes, etc. is all baked into the price of rent. Sometimes this is true. But usually not.

J) **Psychology**. Look at your personal reasons for wanting to own. Do you feel like you can't accomplish something in life until you own a house? Do you feel like it's part of getting married and "Settling down", i.e. creating a nest for your future children? For you, is it a part of becoming an adult. Is this what your parents taught you? Examine the real reasons you want to own and make sure they are coming from a good spot in your heart.

K)   **Your time**. Do you really want to spend all that time working on your house? Is this where your time is best spent towards creating a happy and fulfilled life for yourself?

L)   **Choices**. I feel when I rent I always have the choice to leave. To live wherever in the world I want whenever I want. Adventure becomes a possibility even if I never take advantage of it.

M)   **Stress**. For me (not for everyone) owning a home equals stress. I saw what my parents went through at their worst moments owning a home. I saw what I and others went through in the Internet bust when I first owned a home. I saw what people went through in 2008. People were killing themselves. I don't like that sort of stress. This is how I deal with stress.

N)   **Cash is king**. I like cash in the bank. I like having access to it. I don't like it all tied up in one illiquid investment. I want to fill a bathtub with all the dollar bills I would've used as a down payment on a house. I want to bathe in that bathtub. I'm going to do that later today in fact.

By the way, I do think housing stocks might at different points be a good investment, even now as I write this book, but owning a home is not the best way to invest in housing.

Because this also is part of the American Mythology which we need to break free from in order to free our minds to explore the other opportunities in front of us.

CHAPTER FIFTEEN
What it Feels Like to Be Rich

After losing over one million a week, cash, for the entire summer of 2000, I was forced to sell my apartment. So one day in 2002, all the boxes were packed, the apartment was empty. We had two moving trucks waiting downstairs to move us an hour north of the city. It was like an exile. My self-esteem was gone, my apartment was gone, I hadn't slept a full night in almost three years, and other things I can't even talk about. My ex-wife, my two toddler girls, and Lynne, a close family friend who was helping us move, were taking one last look around. "Oh. My. God," Lynne said: "This is really it."

It's been a decade and a lot has happened, good and bad (mostly good). Someone on Quora yesterday asked the question, "What does it feel like to be rich?" I figured I'd answer based on my pre-2000 experiences. I'll save 2000-2010 for another time.

A lot of people started answering the Quora question with "I was able to buy this, or that, or 'this and that'. " Money was never about that for me, then or now. There's never been anything I wanted to buy (other than the next I-pad!) I have minimal material possessions. If you know me you'd see I dress like crap and the edges of all of my pants are frayed. I don't own a suit. I don't have a driver's license so fancy cars are out. I like comic books more than paintings. I don't like to fly or sail. And I don't drink wine or eat out a lot. So what did it mean for me back then?

- **DNA**. I finally felt good enough about myself to pass on my genes and have children. I never wanted to have children before that. There's apparently some evolutionary reason that we feel a strong urge to pass on our genes. I had never felt that before but somehow having a significant amount of money gave me permission to want to have kids.

-        **Safety**. For the briefest of moments, I felt "safe" – like nothing could harm me and I could live forever. In 1999 I visited the Chairman of a company I was a shareholder of. I was in LA and he picked me up at the hotel in his latest Porsche. We drove to his enormous house and he gave me a tour. When we sat down he told me, "I don't even have to do this anymore. I have so much money now that nothing can touch me." I know it sounds unbelievable and a cliché but a year later he came down with cancer. After battling with cancer for years he was given worse and worse news about the outlook until eventually he shot himself and his kids found the body. I heard about the news when his wife called everyone in his address book. This is not meant to be a lesson. Money has its benefits but immortality is not one of them.

Another example. A friend of mine was running a prominent gaming site and wanted to maybe sell it or do something with (it was 1999, so why not?) I introduced him to a successful guy I knew on Wall Street. I couldn't even find the guy's office. I had never been down as south as Wall Street. My friend and I sat there while Shlomo (not his real name, but you get the drift) said: "look at me! Ten years ago I was a shlub. Now I have 100 million dollars. Only in America, right?" About two years later Shlomo was in the center of a massive FBI sting involving a currency brokerage he had started that had been simply pocketing investors' money since the 70s. He went to jail. Even my orthodox friends turn away and refuse to talk about him whenever I ask if they knew him.

-        **Scarcity**. My feelings of safety and immortality quickly gave way to scarcity. After all, I thought, if I could make 10 million dollars then it must be too easy. In fact, I honestly thought, everyone else had probably already made 11 million dollars. So then I felt poor again. I now needed 100 million dollars to be happy. I drove in a car with a friend of mine and his wife. I said: "everyone has 10 million dollars now." She quickly said: "not everyone".

-       **Friends**. I lost some friends. Then I made some new friends. By the time I was going down in the elevator from my apartment that one last time, 100% of those new friends were destined to never speak to me again (at least through January 12, 2011). My new friends said things like, "Mark Cuban is a stud" or "Fuck him. Take away all his shares" or "Good luck. Have a nice life" or "of course it's legal!"

-       **The value of money**. I realized (too late then, but I learned) that I never knew the value of money. I had never even been aware of money before. My prior goals had been playing games, making fun websites, or writing novels. Now my only goal was money, money, money, and more money. I told my therapist at the time, in 2001, "it's like losing a loved one" and she said: "sweetie, sounds like you've never really lost a loved one before."

Money is a great thing. It's the payoff on hard work, great luck (which is often earned luck) and you can do amazing things with it. Build new businesses, create jobs, buy your independence and freedom from corporate America. But first you have to climb many hurdles, of which earning the money is only the first. Very few things are better than earning a lot of money.

But money finds a home only in places where it's appreciated. I didn't appreciate the money. So it left me.

When we were in the car, driving to our new home back in 2002 it was in the middle of a snowstorm. I wanted to cry I felt so bad about what was happening. But it was too much to think about. So for a brief moment I watched the snow and remembered what it was like to be a kid. Tasting the first snow of the year on the tip of my tongue.

CHAPTER SIXTEEN
How to Turn Your 12 Year Old into an Entrepreneur

One of the most pleasurable days of my life was when my kids picked out items they wanted to sell, put price tags on them, painted signs that they then copied at a copy store and then hung up all over town, and then bargained, negotiated, and made deals left and right until the front of our lawn was empty of all the items they wanted to sell.

Every kid needs entrepreneurial experience. The feeling that you create something powerful enough that people pay money for it. It's exhilarating and inspires growth in so many ways. But it's not about reading, or studying, or being smart, or even providing a good role model. The only way your kid will be an entrepreneur is if he or she starts TODAY.

Keep it simple. Here's some businesses they can start right now:

Idea #1: The Lawn Store:

A)   Tell them to find 10-50 things in their bedroom close that they would be willing to sell. (and believe me, they have those items)

B)   Pick a day to do a garage sale

C)   Have them make the signs for the sale and then they should hang them up all over town. Teach them how to be marketers with these signs. They should be as salesy and noticeable as possible.

D)   Tell them to call all their friends to come over for the garage sale with their parents.

E)   They should organize the items by category. Make them really think about the shopping experience as people mill through the items.

F)   Have them be the salesperson at their garage sale. Negotiate every deal.

Repeat one month later and see how they've learned from the experience. Maybe add a new twist. See if any local stores want to donate items. You can donate the proceeds to charity. Having quality store items will add value to your kid's items. Have your kids do all the bookkeeping. Understand which categories sold best and to what types of customers (did kids buy? Or parents?). Serve coffee so parents can chat and drink while their kids shop. An entire book can be written about kids garage sales. After sale #2, have the kids brainstorm about how sale #3 can be even better. Send me the ideas they come up with.

Idea #2. Newspaper:

Have them make a newspaper of all local news. Sales at local stores, news from neighbors, real estate news, etc. Have them sell the newspaper door to door. Make sure they do at least 2 editions before they lose interest. On second edition they can get sponsors from local stores.

Idea #3: Niche Blog:

Make it a niche blog/newspaper: all the real estate sales and prices in the past six months in your area. They can get the data from the local city clerk. Real estate agents can sponsor the blog if it gets traffic. They can make flyers they can drop off at every house: "Check out local trends in real estate values at this blog", etc. Include their cute picture on the flyer.

Idea #4: Be a consultant.

Go up and down Main Street in your town with your kids. Tell them to come up with 3 ideas for how each store can attract more customers or improve your business. Then have your kid go inside and make an appointment with the owner to share the ideas. For a regular fee (or free cookie), your kid should offer to come back and give more advice. I know this sounds above and beyond (what store owner would care what a kid has to say) but it's a valuable experience for the kids (overcomes shyness, talking to adults, makes them think as a businessperson thinks) but you never know. Could be a good source of free cookies at the local cookie store. I've done this with my kids since they were 5 years old and they've successfully predicted quite a few local bankruptcies (most notably the business, "Balls & Dolls", a store that did exactly what it said. They sold balls (like soccer balls) and dolls (for the kid sisters of the boys who wanted to buy soccer balls).

Idea #5: Blogmaster.

Help other kids set up their first blogs. Charge a small fee. First, of course, your kids should set up their own blogs. What's their favorite topic? Upload a picture. Start blogging. Post on other blogs often enough that they then feel comfortable putting links in their comments back to their own blog, etc. Once your kid has become comfortable with the blog space, make a little brochure, print business cards, and help other kids set up their blogs.

Idea #6: they write a book:

"100 ways 12 year old kids can start businesses" and they sell it via Google ads (or they research other kinds of online marketing).

Idea #7: Stock market:

Give them $100. Tell them they can pick 10 stocks. $10 each. The stock picks have to come from their personal experience (DIS vs. CBS, for instance). They need to diversify: Media, Clothes, Food, etc. Hedge their bets by shorting SPY. Tell them you'll split the profits with them each week. They must have three bullet points per pick and they need to list also what could go wrong with the investment. They need to report back each day how their investments are doing.

Not every kid would want to do these ideas. There has to be a passion underneath. If you want more ideas, let me know. I have some. If you want to send me additional ideas, please post them in the comments on my blog at jamesaltucher.com. Note: I think "learning by watching you" is not a good way to get them to be an entrepreneur. They don't need role models now. They need to just do it.

Don't forget to teach your kids to learn from their failures. If the garage sale doesn't go well, then why? Figure it out and try again. Persistence is everything, whether you are a 12 year old entrepreneur, or an 80 year old one.

On a somewhat controversial note: I sometimes pay my kids to do their homework. I think kids should get used to the idea early on that if they do good work, they get paid for it. Every kid hates homework so it's not like I'm getting in the way of a legitimate passion. So might as well use money to see how it focuses them. They are going to have to learn that sooner or later anyway so the earlier the better.

CHAPTER SEVENTEEN
Osama Stockpickr, and the Art of Negotiation

When the FBI came to my door in mid-2002 and asked me what I knew about "UBL", their name for Osama Bin Laden, I got a bit nervous. My kids were playing on the floor and I was in the middle of trade during a rough patch in the markets. At that time (the Internet Bust) I rarely had anyone who wanted to speak to me at all, particularly the FBI, and everyone in the house at the time wondered if maybe I was in trouble.

But, in a roundabout way I'll explain, all of this brings me to memories of walking around an antique coin show a few years earlier with Dr. Larry Brilliant and discussing the best techniques for negotiation.

I'm a horrible negotiator. I think most people think they are good negotiators, with natural-born talent. This is like the statistic that nine out of ten people think they are above average drivers (only 4 out of ten can really be considered to be above average). I'm the one out of ten that knows he's a poor driver. And I know I'm a poor negotiator. Part of this is because I do consider myself a good salesman. I like people to like me, and to get them to say "yes" as quickly as possible when I'm selling them something (a service, a product, a business, a deal, etc. - I've sold everything possible for every imaginable price). But negotiators aren't necessarily eager to please. Sometimes they are exact opposite.

Fortunately I've learned from the absolute best negotiators ever. And every negotiator has a different technique. Here are some of I've seen in action. First off, there are the basics, which I won't go over too much because everyone knows them. And then there are the three killer techniques.

Basic Negotiation 101

- **Have a backup**: "This price sounds fine to me but I have to ask my board of directors, my partners, my best friend, my CEO, etc." Always have someone you HAVE to go back to who can then throw a wrench in the middle if need be.

- **Never be the first to throw out a price**. This sounds easy in theory but is not practical since everyone knows it. Instead, using the Killer techniques below, you can get around this approach and throw out a first price without fear.

- **Don't be afraid to say NO**: But there's a more useful way of saying this, which is, diversify your choices. This isn't always possible but try not to enter into a negotiation unless you have at least one satisfactory other choice. This applies to everything from dating, to selling your house, to selling your company, to providing a service. Makes it much easier to say: "NO".

- **Both sides need to be happy at the end**. Otherwise, the deal will end up poorly for everyone.

But using the Killer techniques below, everyone should be happy at the end.

Advanced Negotiation 201

- **The Nicker-and-Dimer**. I once went to an ancient coin exhibit with the Dr. Larry Brilliant mentioned above (I know. It's like a name out of a science fiction novel but that's his name). He was former CEO of Softnet, a company that did a bunch of tech stuff until the tech boom ended. Then he was head of Google Charities. Before all of that he cured smallpox in India. Now I have no idea what he does.

The last time we spoke was in 2001, but for various reasons, in 2002 he mentioned to the FBI I might have some good ideas about tracking down "UBL". Anyway, we were shopping for ancient Israeli coins together and he told me this: When you are negotiating, always have more items on your negotiating list than the other guy. If you are selling your company, it's not just about the price of the company. It's about the size of the earn-out, the goals that need to be achieved, salary, salaries for your employees, free car service forever, what's your title, what are your responsibilities, etc. Have more items because then when it gets down to the nut-and-bolts negotiation you can give up the nickels and take the dimes. Then it seems like the other guy is winning but you're still getting everything you really want.

- **The Idiot**. I was once partners in a VC fund with a guy who was an ex managing director at CS First Boston. He had negotiated hundreds of leverage finance deals. He was a genius negotiator and everyone liked doing business with him (which is hard for me to pull off when I'm negotiating). His favorite technique in the middle of a negotiation would be to raise his hands up in the air and say, "Listen. Let's take a step back here. Pretend I'm a complete idiot and walk me through this deal."

He had no fear pretending he was the dumbest guy in the room even though he was probably the smartest. And he would ask any question he wanted and everyone liked being smart in front of him by answering in as much detail as possible. Then he would say "OK, I think I get it but I'm not sure. I need to spend a few days thinking about it." He would completely slow the pace down. And then on every item he would add more tiny items (the nickel and dime approach) and would just wear everyone down. it was almost like taking the nickel-and-dime approach to an extreme. And he was never afraid to say, "OK, it's no big deal. We all have other choices." He was fearless without seeming like he was BS-ing, even though he was always BS-ing (not totally true. We did have other choices but not as good as the one he was negotiating).

- **The Math Trick**. This is the best technique I've seen. This one is from Steve Elkes, former COO of iVillage when he sold it to GE for $500mm. He was then COO of Thestreet.com and managed to rise over $50mm from TCV at a price of $14.26 per share. I don't think the stock ever ticked higher than that (it's in the $2s now). He also negotiated for Thestreet.com when they bought Stockpickr.com, a company I started, so I was able to see his negotiating first hand and unfortunately for me, he was on the other side of the table.

"The Math" technique is this: before the negotiation even begins, you state what you think a common sense, very straightforward, mathematical formula that everyone should use to value the property, service, business, etc.

So for Stockpickr, Thestreet.com was trading for 20 times next year's earnings. So Thestreet needs to buy things where it has upside, Steve said. How about we all agree to pay 10 times next year's earnings for Stockpickr.

I immediately said yes since I had modeled out what I thought were enormous earnings for Stockpickr.com based on the advertising rates Thestreet.com was charging customers, average advertising rates in the industry, the rate our traffic was growing, other revenue opportunities, etc. No problem! I said and thought this was a no-brainer. I was counting the money.

Until bit by bit my number was notched down: advertising rates weren't high as I thought. Steve would then use "The Idiot" technique. "I don't know what advertising rates really are," he said, "so how about we just talk to the head of sales here and see." So then it's suddenly out of both our hands and in the hands of an impartial guy who carefully explained to me why advertising rates weren't as high as they seemed.

Then he used "the backup technique": "I'm fine paying whatever, but the board doesn't see those other revenue opportunities you mention so we have to stick with the revenues and earnings we KNOW you're going to get." And since we had a formula we already agreed to, I was whittled down to agree to the number that the formula spat out. Which was fine. By the end of the negotiation, both sides were happy. I was happy because the initial price I had in my head had slid down so much I was just glad the slide was over. They were happy because they got down to the price they wanted.

As for the FBI agents, Larry Brilliant had mentioned to them an idea I had mentioned to him a few years earlier about a company where I thought Bin Laden was keeping some of his money. Nice guys and seemed like they were on top of it. Eight years later UBL has still not been found.

CHAPTER EIGHTEEN
My Name is James A. and I am an Alcoholic

It was my first meeting of Alcoholics Anonymous. I went to the meeting at that church at the corner of Wall Street and Broadway. I think it's the oldest church in the country. Or the city. Or the "oldest" "something"of "somewhere". We were in the basement and donuts were served. There were about six rows of seats and a dozen or so people were randomly spaced out on them, as if none of us could get too close to each other.

We went up and down the rows introducing ourselves. When it came to me I wasn't sure what to say. I had never been to a meeting before so I more or less copied everyone else. "My name is James and this is my first day of no alcohol." At that, everyone gave a little bit of a clap. "Welcome, James". The leader of the meeting said.

The thing is, I wasn't an alcoholic. I didn't drink at all. And I really didn't want to go to this particular meeting. To make it even worse, an astrologer had told me to go to a 12 step meeting of Business Owners Debtors Anonymous (BODA). But there were no BODA meetings that day so she said: "go to an AA meeting instead. They are all the same." But they weren't all the same. What are you supposed to say if you are not an alcoholic and now it's your turn to speak? I felt like a secret agent behind the Iron Curtain. But I liked the clapping. I felt some pleasure at being so welcomed. But I also felt a little guilty and when the meeting was over I ran away.

A few weeks later I found a BODA meeting to go to at a church on 31st and 7th. Everyone was sitting around in a circle. I liked that. I felt we could all go around in a circle telling stories about ourselves. Like Show-n-Tell in 1st grade. I felt like my show-n-tell would be better than anyone else's. I was there for ego purposes. I wanted all of the other kids in the circle to love me. The truth of the matter even here, though, was that I was neither a business owner at this time, nor a debtor. But here I was, at business owner's debtors anonymous. I also was under the delusion that all of these people needed my help. That I had something to teach them.

People started telling their stories. One woman I remember said: "the good thing is that since I've been going to these meetings is that I don't need as much money."

What!?

At the time, I didn't necessarily think that was such a good thing. I felt like she was just fooling herself. Of course she needed a billion dollars. She was being hypnotized into settling for less. I didn't think she was a "loser" but maybe I was thinking only one level higher than that.

There was one real pretty girl in the BODA meeting. I aimed my story at her. I told the whole thing. I expected intense clapping and whistling at the end but there was none of that and people just went on to the next person. When it was the pretty girl's turn she talked about how she was in intense debt, she didn't like her employer, but she had done something 'so horribly shameful [she] couldn't even admit it in BODA'.

We were all sort of silent then. I'm sure all of us were thinking the same thing. She was wearing a short skirt. What could she have done? I was insanely turned on by her. But then the group went onto the next person.

I can't remember anything else about the meeting. After the meeting was over, the pretty girl disappeared. People

were milling around talking but nobody really talked to me
at all so I left.

Outside of the meeting I had one of the weirdest
coincidences for me ever. About two years earlier I had
invested $300,000 in a company called (don't laugh)
gooey.com. They were an Israeli company and I ended up
on the board of directors of the company. Try not to go on
the board of directors of an Israeli company. By the time
the experience was over it was so bad I thought I was even
going to have to sue myself.

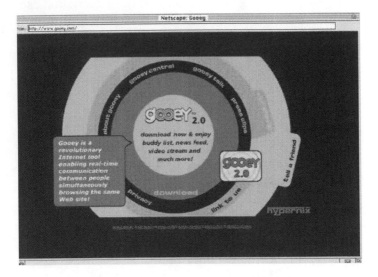

They had software that would turn web pages into chat
rooms. So if I had the gooey software downloaded and you
did also and we were both on the same web page then we
would be able to see each other via the software and start
chatting. In other words, everyone visiting
jamesaltucher.com right now would be able to see each
other and start IMing through gooey about why they were
all here at the same time. I thought this was the "new new
thing" in instant messaging. I put in $300,000 and I got a
bunch of other people to put in about $700,000. Two years

later gooey.com declared bankruptcy. And about three months after that I found myself in my first AA meeting.

So right after I left the BODA meeting there was a homeless guy sitting about a half block from the church. I'm not exaggerating when I say he was lying in his own urine. I'm not exaggerating when I say, coming out of this BODA meeting where I just described, among other things, losing $300,000 on this company, this homeless man lying in his urine was wearing a gooey.com t-shirt. The shirt had a very distinctive logo and colors. I went right up to the guy to make sure I was seeing it correctly.

It was definitely the gooey shirt. I felt like God was sending me a message. I still don't know what to make of the coincidence. I had never even seen anyone other than myself wearing the t-shirt before. I left the man a $20 dollar bill. I don't think he noticed. [As a side note, every single thing I write in this book is dead true. Please don't even comment that this story is not true. Although if I must be honest I don't remember if it was a $20 dollar bill or a ten dollar bill I left with the guy but I'm guessing the higher.]

About a year earlier Gooey had an offer to be acquired for about $100 million from Star Media, the Latin American portal company. I would've made about $4 million on the deal. This was the peak of the bubble. I was begging the company to take the offer. I arranged for the deal to be entirely hedged with a collar put on by Morgan Stanley (dba Justin Weil, "the mad collarer") the second the deal closed so the Star Media stock would be as good as cash.

I visited with the top guys in the company. They were in a random apartment one of them had rented on the west side. At the time their software had about a million downloads but no revenues. "We don't want Star Media!" they told me. "We're Gooey! We want someone prestigious like

Yahoo!" Israelis playing video games while discussing $100 million acquisitions always talk with exclamation points. Otherwise I wouldn't be so liberal in their use. So that deal went down the toilet. As did another potential deal gooey had with the company that is now SIGA Technologies for $150 million. A year later they were bankrupt.

I barely remember the AA meeting, and I only feel mild disappointment now when thinking about what could've been with a Star Media acquisition. Things have worked out for the best in my life without that $4 million I would've made on the deal. Thank god they didn't take it. And 12 years later I even managed to convince myself to invest in another Israeli company. I got over my hatred of Israeli entrepreneurs. I love them now. And I relish coincidences. The homeless guy in the Gooey t-shirt can only be topped if I tell you it was also raining outside, which it was, and I had no umbrella, which I didn't, so I was completely soaked, staring at my $300,000 literally down the drain in a pool of urine, and I was thoroughly depressed.

But not because of this homeless guy.

I knew that all the coincidences in the world were not going to make my dream that evening come true. Because the pretty girl who sat across from me in the BODA meeting had just confessed in the meeting to doing "the most shameful thing I had ever done".

And in my imagination I saw us twenty years later, all our worries behind us, smiling into each other's faces in our cozy house with a fireplace and maybe some kids running around. And maybe right when she was about to drift off into blissful sleep that night twenty years in the future she would finally whisper into my ear, and I would barely be able to hear her – she would finally tell me the shameful secret she had been holding back from me after all of these years.

Side note: What did Gooey and I do wrong?

1.   Not take the offer when it was given. They were offered a ton of money for a company with no revenues. Always take the offer. Make a billion on your next company.

2.   I made the mistake of investing in a team with no prior experience in building and selling a company. I've never done that again.

3.   I didn't have good co-investors with me when I invested in Gooey

4.   I was conflicted because I was also building their website at the time, with my first company, Reset. So part of the money they raised from me personally, went to my company (which had already been acquired so I didn't benefit. So I was serving two masters. Bad idea.

5.   I had no sense before I invested that the Gooey product would be interesting to people. It's hard for any random web page to accumulate enough people at a time to make for an interesting chat.

6.   I had no real say when it came down to a critical decision. No other advocates on my side. I should've been lining up supporters all along within the company to sell when an offer was made. This was late 1999. It was the last chance to take such an offer.

CHAPTER NINETEEN
25 Unusual Ways to Find Abundance

I hate self-help books. And any books or articles or "Rich Dad, Poor Dad" (or "Power of Now") stuff that don't really speak from experience and don't really give you specific steps towards achievement. When you have a gun to your head, with two kids, a mortgage, and your entire self-esteem at risk, you need PRACTICAL methods for moving forward. And you need them from someone who can speak from experience and say, "this works."

Practical doesn't mean: "incorporate your company, hire programmers, etc." And it doesn't mean "appreciate the moment". Once that moment is over you have the rest of your life to worry about. Practical means building the basic foundation that I know for a fact creates wealth. I've had the gun to my head. And it even fired. But I dodged the bullet because of the below.

Claudia, my wife, recently wrote a similar article on her blog, and I am re-writing it with my take:

1)   **Find Your Passion**. This is very hard. The first step is doing the Daily Practice I outlined a few chapters ago. But, to summarize, you need to be healthy (you can't be passionate if you're sick all the time). You need no emotional drama in your life. Zero! You need to keep the idea muscle from atrophying. And you need to have some sort of spiritual practice. This Daily Practice above is the Starting Point for finding your passion. And only the starting point.

2)   **Trust**. This is similar to "giving". You need to share your ideas for free, trusting that the returns to you will be worth much more than if anyone steals your ideas. Ideas need to mate with other ideas to generate children. It's

those children and their descendants that become the real ideas that drive the next generation of innovation. In order for your ideas to mate, you need to trust sharing them with others.

3) **Learn to Receive**. Claudia mentions this as being able to "take a compliment" which is true. But one step further: learn to accept the fact that you don't need to move up linearly in salary at your job. If you follow the Daily Practice and begin to generate value through ideas, and learn to promote yourself (see below), then your value to your organization (or, most likely, any other organization but the one you are currently with) goes up exponentially if you learn how to promote your ideas.

4) **Bless that which you want**. This is Claudia's polite way of saying, "Don't be jealous". I read a story as a kid: two people were walking by the executive dining room at their corporation. One guy said: "look at those jerks. Eating in their own lunchroom." And the other guy said, "I'm fine with them eating there. I'm going to eat there one day." Never be jealous of what you want. It puts a huge dividing line between you and THEM. Admiring the qualities you want to achieve instead of being jealous of them is the only way to achieve them. Catch yourself today anytime you are jealous of people who have more. Reverse it. Build that into your daily practice.

5) **Prayer**. This does not mean "pray to god" (although it could). For me it means spending a few seconds devoting yourself to something other than your base needs and desires. For me, it's sometimes as simple as repeating to myself when I wake up, "Help me save at least one life today." Which has some arrogance in it (I pretend I'm a superhero) but the basic motive is the same - the first goal of the day is to help someone other than myself. Every day I know I'll be a superhero and save at least one life. But the key is to look for the opportunity. Keep your eyes open

all day for that life you need to save. Else someone will die.

6)   **Visualization**. If you visualize you're rich, you won't necessary get rich. But if you constantly visualize you're poor, it's certain you will have such an overwhelming feeling of scarcity that you won't be able to overcome. I have problems with a "scarcity complex". I've sold three profitable businesses and I always joke I'm the only guy who ever sold an internet company on the basis of a multiple of earnings (as opposed to the super-inflated valuations everyone else gets). It's hard for me to step up and really say I deserve more. Visualizing the life you want and deserve is a good way to prepare for those moments where you have a real opportunity to make the leap to that life instead of settling for less. One way to visualize is, of course, with a list. Make a list of the 10 things you want in your life by next year. Visualize how those things can happen. And then take one step forward today towards achieving those things. I try to do this every day and it works. Today I'm going to try and find one more high-traffic place to syndicate my columns.

7)   **Meditation**. This goes hand in hand with visualization. And it's important. Without getting into the specifics of meditation you want to clear your head of the non-stop chatter that gets in the way of your success. Clearing the head lets ideas from the subconscious get closer to the conscious mind. It helps the ideas from one part of your brain mate with ideas from the other part. It's also good practice for getting your mind back into focus during the day when those inevitable "scarcity complex" moments come up where you feel undeserving of the riches you are destined to get. I often find myself in the "Why me" syndrome. Building a meditation practice is good practice for pulling your head back during those moments.

8)   **Studying a spiritual text**. There's been a million bands created since 1960. But only a handful of bands have withstood the test of time so we still listen to them today. The Beatles. Pink Floyd. U2, etc. Similarly, there's been millions of prophets, self-help gurus, advice columns, etc. since 5000 BC but only a few have withstood the test of time. Buddha, Lao Tzu, Confucius, Jesus, and a handful of others. Why did they withstand the test of time? Who knows? But that's why they are worth reading. A little bit each day. Currently I am reading Karen Armstrong's book "12 Steps to a Compassionate Life", which surveys many of the major philosophies.

9)   **Trust, part II**. If something happens, and you've been following the core Daily Practice mentioned above, then trust that things are going in the right direction. In 2009 I started a company, 140Labs. We were going to make twitter-related sites. For instance, we made 140love.com, a dating site for twitter. I had a first round of $500,000 raised and mostly wired in. The morning we were going to close the round I had an overwhelming feeling that this was not a good idea and not how I wanted to spend the next three years of my life. My body was physically shaking as I woke up. So I trusted that moment. I returned the money that had been sent in, canceled the raise, shut down the company (you can still see 140love.com), and moved on, at about $50,000 personal expense to myself. Trusting yourself and the cues your body and mind are telling you despite great grief it could cause (partners, investors, etc. were disappointed in me, not to mention my bank account) is the best way to find success. I ended up having a great year despite that loss of money and time.

10)   **Giving**. See the chapter Give and You Shall Receive

11)   **Say Yes**. In an article I recently wrote I mentioned I always say "No" to anything I don't want to do. But, with

an important caveat. I almost always say "Yes" to new experience, even to the point of throwing myself into that experience. That's how stories are generated, that's how real knowledge is generated so new ideas can be formed with your old ones. This is how life becomes interesting. I never wanted to go to India before in my life. Last month I went and it was well worth it. I always look forward to meeting new people. And I always look forward to the next surprise I say "Yes" to.

Don't forget: for our whole lives everyone around us gave us great examples about what it looks like to be "unhappy". Now you have to say "Yes" to happiness. It's hard because nobody taught us how to. That's why you have to say "Yes" to new experiences. Since each new thing might teach us that elusive happiness. .

12)   **Learn the value of money**. Don't be frivolous. Don't be extravagant. Don't assume other people have money. Don't change your life at all when you make money. See later chapter "What to do after you make a Zillion Dollars"

13)   **Bless Money**. You always hear, "money is the root of all evil". It's actually not. Money creates jobs, creates products that improve the quality of life, money can be given to charity, money can be given to our children so they hopefully live better lives than we did. Money can be used to pay for healthcare for ourselves and our family. My biggest regret in life is during a low point, not having the money I felt was required to really help my dad recover from a stroke. I'm devastated by that still. Money doesn't solve all of your problems, but it does solve your money problems.

14)   **Be grateful**. Exercise your idea muscle right now. Can you think of 32 things you are grateful for? Can you do that again every day? I find this to be a useful prayer.

15) **Do yoga.** This is from Claudia's post. At the very least, exercise is important for three important reasons:

1. All evidence suggests that people who exercise live longer.

2. You'll be more confident and it will show

3. When you exercise you often have to deal with short-term situations when your body is in extreme pain. You have to breathe through those situations (whether it's yoga, lifting weights, doing 100 pushups, shooting baskets, etc.). this is great practice for breathing through those difficult situations that often come up in life.

Yoga specifically I find to be very interesting. It exercises the muscles. It's continuous (so a half hour yoga session is often equivalent to a 1 hour gym session where there are breaks between using the different machines) and it forces you to breathe deeply in often incredibly difficult-to-get-into positions, a necessary tool for life. Additionally, breathing in those positions forces oxygen into parts of your body that are not used to it.

16) **Dedication.** Part of my prayer in the morning of "Save a life" is I dedicate my day to a "higher power". I hate using that word. It sounds like a new age phrase. But whatever. Call it "The Force". It's not so bad to try and imagine the Force working through you. Try it for a day or two.

17) **Add value to others**. This is part of the "give" point above but deserves its own point. It's a rule of the universe that you can only create value for yourself if you stridently attempt to create even more value for others. The only way

I've ever made money was by creating something that had lasting value for others. Every other attempt at a shortcut failed miserably.

18) **Offer for free**. I always want to be as honest as possible. If I'm offering something for free, there's no bullshit. I don't have to convince anyone of anything. It's free. Either take it or not. Then, if people take it, I learn from it, the ideas get better, the service improves, I get to know the audience better, word of mouth gets better, etc. Even in a consulting business, get your foot in the door with such good ideas that the door becomes wide open. Then you can charge. I once had a client that I visited once a month for over a year before I made a single dime off of him. Then, in one chunk, I made $750,000 from him. As the great Barry Ritholz has told me, "Never let a whale off the hook".

19) **Learn to charge for services**. When I started a company building websites the hardest part was learning how to charge. I quickly found out I was charging about 1/100 of what my competitors were charging (Razorfish, Agency.com, etc.) and was able to adjust accordingly. But it was hard. I'm a salesman. So my whole goal was to always close the deal and get the client to say "Yes". The lower the price, the easier to get them to say "yes" (in most cases). Learning to balance this has been my life-long challenge.

20) **Promote yourself**. This is easy advice but hard to follow. How do you promote yourself? One thing is by learning how to write. Most bloggers/businessmen out there don't know how to write. I would say on a scale of 0 to 10 most people are a 1 at best. The first step in promoting yourself, believe it or not, is reading high quality writing. Read stories by Raymond Carver, essays by David Foster Wallace or Malcolm Gladwell. Read as much good writing as you can get your hands on. You

need to be able to express yourself in order to promote yourself. In order to express yourself well you need to be a good writer and communicator. And don't forget these important rules for good writing:

1.   After you are done with your article, take out the first paragraph and last paragraph. Almost certain that it will read better.

2.   Along those lines, try to take out every other sentence.

3.   Bleed a little in each article/essay/post (i.e. a personal story that shows you're human like the rest of us)

4.   Provide value. Make sure you aren't regurgitating something written somewhere else on the entire World Wide Web. Really create something new. Else, don't write. Never say anything that doesn't add value. Else, you are wasting everyone's time.

And then, key, try to distribute/syndicate in as many places as possible. But only after you have followed the above rules. This will build the ability to promote yourself.

21) **Brush your teeth**. Nobody wants to give money to people with bad breath. It's just a fact of life. The same goes for cleaning up your workspace. And try to dress as cleanly as possible. This is almost impossible for me. I tend to appear disheveled no matter what I do. But I try.

22) **Ask**. When I started my first business, Reset, I asked corporate customers what it is they wanted to achieve with a website. I listened as much as possible without talking. And then I would come back with ideas, hopefully enhancing even further the ideas they had about their own

website presence. Asking, then listening is the first steps towards creating value for someone else. Someone recently wrote me asking me for so-and-so's email address. But in his letter to me he gave no reason why he wanted it, provided no value, and was clearly not concerned with why so-and-so would have any interest in talking to him. So I deleted the email.

23) **Ideas**. I stress this in a billion other posts but specifically, find ten people you want to do business with, list them, then list ten ideas you think can improve their business. Realistically think about how they (or you) can execute on those ideas. They have to be easy to execute. List how they can execute each idea. Do this every day. Whittle down the lists. Send each list out to the people you want to help. Before you know it, you will have a business helping people. This is a guarantee. Helping people is also the fastest way to profits. It's also a guarantee that if you don't exercise that idea muscle, it will atrophy. Quickly.

24) **Laughter**. I give a lot of public talks. I try to follow the 50-50 rule. 50% real value, 50% laughter. Make sure people laugh. Most of the time they only remember what made them laugh. But every now and then real value slips in. How do you make people laugh if you aren't funny? Learn how to be funny:

1. Get a list of funny books and read them. Start with something smart and funny, like Kurt Vonnegut's "Cat's Cradle". Something more contemporary is anything by Nora Ephron or Ariel Leve. Or books by comedians, like Seinlanguage, Jim Norton's books, etc.

2. Watch on YouTube funny standup. Anything. Richard Pryor is great. Seinfeld is great. Anything.

3.   Watch funny movies. My current favorite: "Superbad". My current favorite funny sitcom: "Arrested Development".

4.   There are actual books on how to be funny. "The Standup Bible" (or "Comedy Bible") by Judy Carter is one.

5.   Watch "Jon Stewart". He's the best. Study how he pauses often. Even his silences are funny.

People will want to work with you, buy your company, give you money, etc., if you do the 50-50 rule. Provide value, and make them laugh. A lot of companies can provide value. But you stand out if you can also provide laughter.

25) **Surrender**. You want something. Badly. But if all you do is think about it, you'll never get it. Visualize exactly what it is that you want, and then give it up to the universe that you will get it. I know this again sounds corny, new-agey, but it's on solid ground. If you obsess you'll be too fixated on what you want to be able to change directions at a moment's notice.

Being able to change and trust that the change is correct is critical. In June, 2006, I received an offer for the fund of funds I was running. It was a healthy offer of about 15% of assets when similar companies were being acquired for 3% of assets. Millions of dollars.

But they wanted me to stay locked up for six years. I couldn't sign myself up for slavery. So my business partner and I said "no". Then we wondered, "What the hell?" We just spent several years building up a business that had no equity value unless we agreed to indentured slavery. So we switched directions on the spot. We created several websites, and one after the other, if they didn't take off immediately, we stopped it.

Eventually one took off. Stockpickr.com. But we knew that we were putting in the right effort, the right daily practice, we knew what we wanted, but we had to surrender that the results might not come in the way we expected. The key was to not get disappointed. The way you don't get disappointed along the way is to know that you've surrender to a higher power (or even better, you've surrendered to the fact that your Daily Practice has made you equipped for the long-term to generate success).

The above 25 methods are difficult. Most people can't do them. And don't set yourself up for goals you can't achieve. But a constant attempt to do the above will allow anyone to conquer the obstacles in this way. I don't believe in self-help. But I certainly believe in helping myself. This is the way I do it.

CHAPTER TWENTY

My Worst Experience as an Entrepreneur. Or…How I Screwed Yasser Arafat Out of $2mm while losing another $100mm in the process

I needed to make one hundred million dollars pretty fast. You know how it is. There are bills to pay. There are things you want to do in life. I wanted, for instance, to work as a cashier in a bookstore. But with a twist. I would own the bookstore. I wanted to do a 90 second ad in the SuperBowl which would just be me walking around for 90 seconds saying and doing nothing. People would argue afterwards, "He could've used that money for charity. How selfish!" But I wouldn't care. It was my money and I could do what I want with it. I would be teaching this grand lesson to all the people watching the Superbowl. I had no other specific desires about what I would do with one hundred million dollars. Just those two. But I knew more things would come.

At the time (1999) I had recently made money selling a company in the web services business. Among other things, my company made the website for the movie, "The Matrix". I knew I was Neo but I wouldn't be able to take the red pill until I had my first hundred million. That was the pill that would let me be a real person. The pill that would allow me to be fully alive.

So I came up with an idea. It was a catchphrase and I would use it many times over the next six months. "First there was the wireLINE internet. Then there was the wireLESS internet. Which would be ten times bigger."

Those three sentences (or maybe it's one if you use commas) were my path to $100 million. Here's what you do then once you have your catchphrase. I had a business partner who wasn't shy. So he called up 20 companies in the wireless software business and said, "We want to buy your company." We had no money to buy anybody but if you ever let that slow you down you might as well run around naked in a football stadium with 60,000 people watching you.

One company responded. A company called "MobileLogic" out of Denver. They flew in and we took them out to breakfast at the Royalton Hotel on 44th Street. It's a fancy breakfast place. The sort of place Rupert Murdoch orders the pancakes, chews it up, spit's it out without swallowing, and then orders granola to be healthy.

We're all sitting around a table. "It's fortunate that you called," the CEO of MobileLogic said to us. "Since Ericsson just offered us seventeen million and we're thinking of taking it." "Why would you take that," I said. "We'll offer you twenty million, half cash, half stock. That stock alone will be worth one hundred million or more once we go public. We have five other companies we'll buy after you. You'll be President of a major company that's going public, pronto. Ericsson is the old generation. Be a part of something new and exciting."

I love the pancakes at the Royalton. They whip the eggs into the batter. It's fluffy and delicious. And the bacon is thick and the bacon juices spill into your mouth as you bite into it. Life was good. Jerry Levin might very well have been at the table next to us buying AOL right in front of our eyes. That's how good life was then.

They took our offer. We quickly wrote up a binding LOI which they signed. We negotiated their salaries, their options, their earn out, everything. Now we needed to pay them twenty million dollars. We knew we could pay half the twenty in stock. So that was easy. That was a piece of paper. Now we had to come up with the other ten.

No problem. Because suddenly I had a real asset. I had a binding LOI for a company with $5-10mm in revenues (despite my propensity to remember every detail of my childhood, I can't remember how much in revenues this company I was buying in 1999 had). There were companies going public then with zero dollars in revenues that were now worth over a hundred trillion dollars.

So, with some partners who were excellent middlemen I started going to potential investors. Mark Patterson, who was then vice chairman of CSFB and is now the head of multi-billion dollar hedge fund Maitlin-Patterson set up a conference call with a few small investors. One call he set up was with Henry Kravis, Leo Hindery, Jim McMann (CEO of 1800-Flowers) and Dennis something or other who just sold a huge Irish telecom company and was worth a random billion or so. I gave a fifteen minute talk. I described my background and the company I had sold. Then I used my catchphrase (see above) and scoped out the opportunity ("10x the size of the wireline internet") and that was the call. Henry Kravis asked a question. I can't remember what it was now because all I kept thinking was "you were the barbarian at the gate and now I'm the barbarian."

Right after the call, Mark Patterson's phone started ringing. Mark told me, "Henry wants to wire five million right now." But we only took one from him. Too many other people wanted to invest. Everyone on that 15 minute conference call put in one million each.

At another meeting to raise money, I had to describe what we did. I wasn't even totally sure what MobileLogic did. We protected data that was in corporate databases but was being sent out to the sales forces through wireless devices that we set up. It was pretty solid. I said, "the data goes to the satellite and then comes down to our devices."

"I thought the data didn't go through satellites. Doesn't data go through cellular towers?" someone named Mamoon asked.

Uh-oh. That seemed to make more sense than satellites. "Sometimes," I answered.

And they put five million in. Frank Quattrone put money in. Sam Waksal, Allen & Co. CMGI. The list goes on. We were the hot investment for three seconds. One guy who had initially rejected us but then saw the list of investors called me at two in the morning and said: "please let me put in a million."

So we closed on thirty million dollars and bought our first company. Then we bought a second company. A consulting company called Katahdin. They had nothing to do with wireless but they had profits. We'd bury them in the IPO story but make use of their profits. Then we bought a third company. I can't even remember their name but they were a spinoff from MIT. Right away we were getting calls. Aether Systems wanted to buy us but we said no. They only wanted to pay fifty million for the company. A banker at CS First Boston told us he could get us seventy five million no problem. But we didn't even listen to him. In the elevator we laughed at him. What an old fool! We were going for an IPO.

Every bank came in with a PowerPoint and a team of young people to pitch us. Goldman, CSFB, Merrill, Lehman, etc. CSFB was the front runner because Frank Quattrone was an investor but Merrill made a strong pitch. The pitch was funny. The top Merrill banker was there. He said to the associate on the deal, "John, walk them through

the numbers." And John said, "uhh, my name is Roy".
Two other things I remember from the pitch. The first was,
"Henry Blodget will be the analyst on this deal. He loves
wireless." Which made no sense to me since he was an
Internet consumer analyst.

The other thing I remember was the back page of the
presentation. The beautiful back page. The only page that
mattered. It had what my net worth would be if we IPOed
and the market valued us similar to Aether Systems. I
would be worth something like nine hundred million
dollars.

I knew exactly what bookstore I wanted to buy. It would
be Shakespeare & Company on Broadway. None of the
other employees would know that I would be the owner.
And I would work just stacking books and being the guy at
the cash register. My secret would give me infinite power.

I didn't know how to be CEO of this company. And
because I didn't really know any of the employees of the
companies we were buying I was feeling very shy. I would
call my secretary before I arrived at work and ask her if
anyone was in the hallway and could she please unlock my
office door. Then I would hurry into the office and lock
the door behind me.

Eventually they replaced me as CEO. Even later, when we
had to rise up to another 70 million, they asked me to step
off as a director on the board. At one point I arranged for a
reverse merger to occur. We'd be public at least at a
hundred million dollar valuation. But the guy behind the
reverse merger turned out to have a checkered past and
had spent some time in jail in 1969 for either
embezzlement or something to do with transporting fake
diamonds. But that's another story.

None of this portrays me in a good light at all. Except for maybe the fact that I was a good salesman during the greatest bubble in world history. But it was decade ago and I don't mind what people think.

But I did learn several things that became incredibly important to me later:

A) If you have to raise thirty million to start your business, it's probably not a good business (at least for me). All of my good businesses (businesses that I started that I eventually sold and made money on) started off profitable from day one and never raised a dime of money.

B) Most M&A transactions don't work. When you buy a company, it's very hard to keep the owners of the old company incentivized. 90% of acquisitions don't work. Build your business. Don't buy it.

C) A lesson I learn repeatedly: traveling for business almost never generates more revenues. New York (and America) is big enough a place to generate revenues. You should never travel. In the course of doing this business I traveled repeatedly to the west coast, Denver, England (to try and buy a company), Sweden (where Ericsson was based), Germany (Ericsson wanted me to show up at a conference for one day), Georgia, Florida, Boston, etc. etc. Not a single meeting generated any revenues for the business but wasted hundreds of hours of my life.

D) Hiring smart people doesn't work if you aren't smart. Everything ultimately comes from the top down.

E) Spending a lot of money on branding and marketing materials is a waste of money for a startup. If you don't know who you are, no amount of money will create materials explaining who you are.

F) If you are going to raise thirty million for a business, then raise a hundred million if you can. Don't turn down Henry Kravis's five million. It doesn't matter how badly you get diluted. If you have to raise money, take in every dime you can.

G) **MOST IMPORTANT**: If you raise thirty million, spend none of it. Warren Buffett once said: "if you know a business will be around 20 years from now then it's probably a good investment." With thirty million we could've stayed in business for 20 years or more and eventually figured ourselves out. Instead, I spent forty million in the first month or so. I learned a lot, and over a hundred million was lost.

Eventually Vaultus (the name of the company. I think I forgot to mention it until now) was sold to Antenna Software. I made no money, as I rightfully shouldn't.

Four years later, I was on a train to Boston with my business partner. It was 5 in the morning and we were going up to visit a hedge fund we were invested in. He was reading Bloomberg magazine. "Holy shit," he said, waking me up. He showed me an article in the magazine. It was about Yasser Arafat, who had just died. Turns out he had a front corporation that was making various investments for him from the money he had somehow made off of the PLO. His largest (or second largest) investment was two million dollars he had put into a "New York company, Vaultus, Inc.". I can tell you for a fact his estate lost that two million. So, as they say in Brooklyn, it was good for the Jews.

CHAPTER TWENTY-ONE
33 Unusual Tips for Being a Better Writer

Back in college, Sanket and I would hang out in bars and try to talk to women but I was horrible at it. Nobody would talk to me for more than thirty seconds and every woman would laugh at all his jokes for what seemed like hours. Even decades later I think they are still laughing at his jokes. One time he turned to me, "the girls are getting bored when you talk. Your stories go on too long. From now on, you need to leave out every other sentence when you tell a story." We were both undergrads in Computer Science. I haven't seen him since but that's the most important writing (and communicating) advice I ever got.

You might say, "I don't want to be a novelist, I want to be an entrepreneur." But being an entrepreneur implies you have at least some of the following abilities:

A)   The ability to generate ideas

B)   To communicate those ideas

C)   To convince others of your ideas – whether those others are customers, investors or an eventual buyer of your company.

Each of the tips below will improve you not only as a writer but an entrepreneur.

33 other tips to be a better writer:

-       **Write whatever you want**. Then take out the first paragraph and last paragraph. Here's the funny thing about this rule. It's sort of like knowing the future. You still can't change it. In other words, even if you know this rule and write the article, the article will still be better if you take out the first paragraph and the last paragraph.

- **Take a huge bowel movement every day**. And you won't see that on any other list on how to be a better writer. If your body doesn't flow then your brain won't flow. Eat more fruit if you have to.

- **Bleed in the first line**. We're all human. A computer can win Jeopardy but still not write a novel. You want people to relate to you, then you have to be human. Penelope Trunk started a blog post: "I smashed a lamp over my head. There was blood everywhere. And glass. And I took a picture." That's real bleeding. My wife recently put up a post where the first line was so painful she had to take it down. Too many people were crying.

- **Don't ask for permission**. In other words, never say "in my opinion" (or worse "IMHO"). We know it's your opinion. You're writing it.

- **Write a lot**. I spent the entire 90s writing bad fiction. 5 bad novels. Dozens of bad stories. But I learned to handle massive rejection. And how to put two words together. In my head, I won the Pulitzer prize. But in my hand, over 100 rejection letters.

- **Read a lot**. You can't write without first reading. A lot. When I was writing five bad novels in a row I would read all day long whenever I wasn't writing (I had a job as a programmer, which I would do for about five minutes a day because my programs all worked and I just had to "maintain" them). I read everything I could get my hands on.

- **Read before you write**. Before I write every day I spend 30-60 minutes reading high quality short stories poetry, or essays. Books by Denis Johnson, Miranda July,

David Foster Wallace, Ariel Leve, William Vollmann, Raymond Carver, etc. All of the writers are in the top 1/1000 of 1% of writers. It has to be at that level or else it won't lift up your writing at all.

- **Coffee**. I go through three cups at least before I even begin to write. No coffee, no creativity.

- **Break the laws of physics**. There's no time in text. Nothing has to go in order. Don't make it nonsense. But don't be beholden to the laws of physics

- **Be Honest**. Tell people the stuff they all think but nobody ever says. Some people will be angry you let out the secret. But most people will be grateful. Else you aren't delivering value. Be the little boy in the Emperor Wears No Clothes. If you can't do this, don't write.

- **Don't Hurt Anyone**. This goes against the above rule. But I never like to hurt people. And I don't respect people who get page views by breaking this rule. Don't be a bad guy.

- **Don't be afraid of what people think.** For each single person you worry about, deduct 1% in quality from your writing. Everyone has deductions. I have to deduct about 10% right off the top. Maybe there are 10 people I'm worried about. Some of them are evil people. Some of them are people I just don't want to offend. So my writing is only about 90% of what it could be. But I think most people write at about 20% of what it could be. Believe it or not, clients, customers, friends, family, will love you more if you are honest with them. So we all have our boundaries. But try this: for the next ten things you write, tell people something that nobody knows about you.

- **Be opinionated**. Most people I know have strong opinions about at least one or two things. Write about those. Nobody cares about all the things you don't have strong opinions on. Barry Ritholz told me the other day he doesn't start writing until he's angry about something. That's one approach. Barry and I have had some great writing fights because sometimes we've been angry at each other.

-       **Have a shocking title**. I blew it the other day. I wanted to title the piece: "How I torture women" (see the article at jamesaltucher.com) but I settled for "I'm guilty of torture". I wimped out. But I have some other fun ones. Like "is it bad I wanted my first kid to be aborted" (which the famous Howard Lindzon cautioned me against). Don't forget that you are competing against a trillion other pieces of content out there. So you need a title to draw people in. Else you lose.

-       **Steal**. I don't quite mean it literally. But if you know a topic gets page views (and you aren't hurting anyone) than steal it, no matter who's written about it or how many times you've written about it before.

-       **Make people cry**. If you've ever been in love, you know how to cry. Bring readers to that moment when they were a child, and all of life was in front of them, except for that one bittersweet moment when everything began to change. If only that one moment could've lasted forever. Please let me go back in time right now to that moment. But now it's gone.

-       **Relate to people**. The past decade has totally sucked. For everyone. The country has been in post-traumatic stress syndrome since 9/11 and 2008 only made it worse. I've gone broke a few times during the decade, had a divorce, lost friendships, and have only survived (barely) by being persistent and knowing I had two kids to take care of, and loneliness to fight. Nobody's perfect.

We're all trying. Show people how you are trying and struggling. Nobody expects you to be a superhero.

- **Time heals all wounds**. Everyone has experiences they don't want to write about. But with enough time, it's OK. An article I wrote: My New Year's Resolution of 1995 is pretty embarrassing. But, whatever. It's 16 years ago. The longer back you go, the less you have to worry about what people think.

- **Risk**. Notice that almost all of these rules are about where the boundaries are. Most people play it too safe. When you are really risking something and the reader senses that (and they WILL sense it), then you know you are in good territory. If you aren't risking something, then I'm moving on. I know I'm on the right track if after I post something someone tweets, "OMFG".

- **Be funny**. You can be all of the above and be funny at the same time. When I went to India I was brutalized by my first few yoga classes (actually every yoga class). And I was intimidated by everyone around me. They were like yoga superheroes and I felt like a fraud around them. So I cried, and hopefully people laughed. (See article: "How Yoga Totally Humiliated Me", at JamesAltucher.com) It was also a case where I didn't have to dig into my past but I had an experience that was happening to me right then. How do you be funny? First rule of funny: ugly people are funny. I'm naturally ugly so it's easy. Make yourself as ugly as possible. Nobody wants to read that you are beautiful and doing great in life.

- **The last line needs to go BOOM!** Your article is meaningless unless the last line KILLS. Read the book of short stories "Jesus' Son" by Denis Johnson. It's the only way to learn how to do a last line. The last line should take you all the way back to the first line and then "BOOM!"

-      **Use a lot of periods**. Forget commas and semicolons. A period makes people pause. Your sentences should be strong enough that you want people to pause and think about it. This will also make your sentences shorter. Short sentences are good.

-      **Write every day**. This is a must. Writing is spiritual practice. You are diving inside of yourself and cleaning out the toxins. If you don't do it every day, you lose the ability. If you do it every day, then slowly you find out where all the toxins are. And the cleaning can begin.

-      **Write with the same voice you talk in**. You've spent your whole life learning how to communicate with that voice. Why change it when you communicate with text?

-      **Deliver value with every sentence**. Even on a tweet or Facebook status update. Deliver poetry and value with every word. Else, be quiet.

-      **Take what everyone thinks and explore the opposite**. Don't disagree just to disagree. But explore. Turn the world upside down. Guess what? There are people living in China. Plenty of times you'll find value where nobody else did.

-      **Have lots of ideas**. I discuss this in "How to be the Luckiest Person Alive" in the Daily Practice section. Your idea muscle atrophies within days if you don't exercise it. Then what do you do? You need to exercise it every day until it hurts. Else, no ideas.

-      **Sleep eight hours a day**. Go to sleep before 9pm at least 4 days a week. And stretch while taking deep breaths before you write. We supposedly use only 5% of our brain. You need to use 6% at least to write better than everyone else. So make sure your brain is getting as much healthy oxygen as possible. Too many people waste valuable writing or resting time by chattering until all hours of the night.

- **Don't write if you're upset at someone**. Then the person you are upset at becomes your audience. You want to love and flirt with your audience so they can love you back.

- **Use "said" instead of any other word**. Don't use "he suggested" or "he bellowed". Just "he said." We'll figure it out if he suggested something.

- **Paint**. Or draw. Keep exercising other creative muscles.

- **Let it sleep**. Whatever you are working on, sleep on it. Then wake up, stretch, coffee, read, and look again. Rewrite. Take out every other sentence.

- **Then take out every other sentence again**. Or something like that.

Sanket didn't want to go to grad school after we graduated. He had another plan. Let's go to Thailand, he said. And become monks in a Buddhist monastery for a year. We can date Thai women whenever we aren't begging for food, he said. It will be great and we'll get life experience.

It sounded good to me.

But then he got accepted to the University of Wisconsin and got a PhD. Now he lives in India and works for Oracle. And as for me, I don't know what the hell happened to me.

CHAPTER TWENTY-TWO
Give and You Will Receive

After a failure I feel lonely and afraid. It's hardest at these moments to pick yourself up and give a little in order to get. The only way to climb out of the hole, when you have a metaphoric needle sticking out of your veins and you're lying in the gutter that the world has kicked you to, is to give back without asking, give as if you were the richest man in the world.

This is not the same as giving to charity. There are so many other ways to give that are underappreciated. But it's exactly these types of giving where the world will give you back ten times more than you gave.

Very important: **the only way you can ever make money is if you provide and add value to others**. That means to succeed as an entrepreneur you have to be in a constant state of "how can I give more" or "how can I help others make even more money" or "How I can I help people to be happier".

Here' s 13 ways that Giving can help you Receive more

- **Give credit where it's due**. Every day, give credit to your boss, your friends, your employees, your colleagues, even if it was your own ideas. Just give them credit. Everyone knows the reality. And the reality is YOU.

- **Give Equity**. When I started Stockpickr, someone wrote a post criticizing me for giving Thestreet.com 50% of my business. One of my employees even quit, he was so upset at that decision. (Although he's since gone on to better things (for example he made the 4-million views viral-video about "The Bernank")). But that decision hooked Thestreet.com into my business. Once the company was up for sale (which was the second after we launched the company) they were basically locked into my tractor beam to the point where they had to buy the company. If I had given them any less of the business I'd probably be sitting on a worthless website right now, post financial crisis.

-        **Give a customer more than they asked for**. When I first did websites for New line cinema (in my old business, Reset), I offered to essentially do websites for all of their movies for almost free. That kept business coming from the whole Time Warner family and also gave my employees fun stuff to do in between doing websites for Con Edison and other boring companies. It also got clients for me because everyone thought our New Line sites were 'edgy'.

-        **Give up**. Some businesses just don't work. Don't make the issue worse by raising money and being fooled by the prophets who tell you persistence is key. 140love.com was my latest bad idea. Go check it out. I put $30k into that baby and on the eve of raising $500k I told everyone to save their wires and not send the money. It was a bad idea. The ghost-site still exists. Knock yourselves out.

-        **Give ideas**. I've told this story before, but when I was really down and wanted to get things going for myself, I came up with as many ideas as I could for other people and simply gave them away for free. The results were stupendous. Sit down every day, picture a person you can give ideas to, and come up with ten good ideas for them. At the very least this will exercise the idea muscle, which atrophies like any other muscle if it's not in constant use.

- **Give time**. Cornell, my alma-mater, recently asked me to donate some money, like they ask all alumni. I said there's no way I can do that since I've repeatedly written articles suggesting that parents not send their kids to college. BUT, I would be more than happy to give my time. So I went up, spoke to a bunch of groups of very smart, talented college students, and even found out about a business done by students who had just graduated that seemed interesting. I immediately came home and invested in the business.

- **Give silence**. My 8 year old was crying the other day. She was upset about nothing. Like 8 year old girls sometimes get. But I sat down next to her and said nothing and just listened while her mind thrashed about a bit. I'm glad I did it. Just to hear her laugh a little by the end of it.

- **Give to yourself**. When I have a score, I give to myself. I'll stay in a nice hotel, or go on a nice trip, or buy some books, or take some time to go to an art gallery or museum. I take for myself when I've been given. Which goes along with…

- **Give thanks**. Every day at the end of the day, I think of the things I'm thankful and grateful for. You don't need to be good at meditation to be as enlightened as the Buddha. Just spend a few minutes a day counting the things you are thankful for. I'm thankful for my family. I'm thankful for the people who have remained friends over the years. I'm also thankful Ben Bernanke decided to print up another $600bb dollars over the next few months. I hope I can take some of that and put it in my pocket.

- **Give for free**. Don't fool yourself into thinking that giving to charity is a good thing. It's a completely selfish act when you give $100 for someone to finish a 100 mile race for charity and you put your name all over the donation. If you really want to "give", do it anonymous and stop waving it in front of our faces.

-       **Give your honesty**. When someone asks for your opinion on something there's so many incentives to lie. When someone asks you to dinner or out to an event, the first impulse is to be dishonest and say: "sorry, my leg is breaking that day, I can't". But be honest and constructive in your honesty. Give value when you give your opinion. Help someone be better by making sure you are not only honest with them but really honest with yourself as to why your opinions are what they are. Where do they come from deep down? Make their lives better and they will one day return the favor. Try being 100% honest for just one day. It's not as easy as it seems. Never criticize but improve the things around you when you give your honesty.

-       **Save a life every day**. I've written about this before. But my goal in life is to be a vigilante, anonymous superhero. If you can save a life a day, with strangers or with friends, then you're a hero. And heroes have all sorts of benefit's in life that civilians never get or don't even know exists. If you don't believe me, save a life today and see what happens.

-       **Meditate on giving**. Above I said give thanks for everything there is to be thankful for. That's one meditation. The other meditation is to think of all the giving you can do tomorrow. Go up and down this list and see what items on it you can do tomorrow.

Give first, then receive. It works.

CHAPTER TWENTY-THREE
What to Do after You Make a Zillion Dollars

In the dot-com boom I made a little bit of money and then proceeded to make every mistake possible with that money. It was like reading a Stephen King horror story written in blood across your bank statement. Several years later, I included the story in the intro to one of my books and gave the book to a potential investor. He read the intro and said, "I can't invest in you. You're a functional idiot." And yet, I've seen the pattern repeated so many times with so many people can I at least enjoy the company of other idiots?

So to help out others who will pocket some of the $600bb in quantitative easing, I have a few simple tips for greatly improving the chances of success if you have sudden fortune thrust upon you, either through your hard work or simply by chance.

1) **The One-Year Rule**. Don't change your lifestyle at all for at least one year.

No new house or apartment. Don't buy a fancy car. Don't buy expensive artwork. This is not to say these things are bad. It's just that you need to let the new wealth marinate your soul a little bit.

Get comfortable with it before you try on new clothes that might not fit yet. Once you buy some massively expensive toys or homes, it changes your whole perspective and might make you much more foolish than you were when you were first climbing the ladder of success.

Remember: One year.

2) **The No-Friends Rule**. Don't lend money to old friends. Don't be so quick to make new friends. Once you make money, everyone will approach you about new investments you can make. Or people will want to borrow money from you.

Don't do either.

It's very hard, of course, to deny a friend who says: "listen, I just need to borrow $100,000 for 90 days." Or "I have a great new start-up that looks like Twitter but better. I'm just raising $500,000 and I left $300,000 for you to come into the round."

But here's what you can say, "I'd love to do it. It sounds great. Right now everything is tied up with my financial adviser and you can talk to him. I have to go by what he says because of all the legal stuff I don't understand." And then get some guy to pretend to be your financial adviser who can get you off the hook by denying your friend.

I know, it's dishonest and devious. But it's necessary in you want to keep your friends. Particularly in Year One (see previous rule).

3) **Don't Invest**. What's the rush? You just made your money. Put it in a savings account for one year at least. Or under your mattress. No stocks. No paintings. No private investments. Try not to start a business again so quickly.

A friend of mine recently won $3 million in a poker tournament after being broke for many years (all his life). Right away he wanted to buy a hotel.

Don't do it.

This was right before the entire housing crisis and recession that followed. Thank God he took my advice. If you feel absolutely compelled to do some investing then follow the next rule.

4) **The 2% Rule**. If you really feel that Google is going to $5,000 per share and you have to buy some stock at $500, don't put more than 2% of your money into it. Then, if it all goes to hell, you've only lost 2% of your money (or more likely, 1%, since Google will probably never go down more than 50%).

This is hard for entrepreneurs who come into sudden wealth because they are used to making their money by having most of their net worth tied up in one investment (their business).

But this is probably the most important rule on the list.

5) **The Good Health Rule**. Believe it or not, your health is now at risk if you just came into sudden wealth.

A friend of mine had a very stressful business in the online gambling space. He was worried the Feds were going to outlaw him and arrest him. He was broke and the business was always in a state of running out of money.

High, high, stress.

I thought he was going to have a stroke or a heart attack but he always stayed in great health. Then he sold his business and made about $50 million. Three months later he was on a ski slope in Aspen, enjoying the fruits of his labor, when he suddenly had a major heart attack and only survived because of immediate medical care. He was essentially dead for five minutes on the operating table.

Your body, in a high adrenalin situation, will postpone punishing you until the situation is over. But don't think when the stress is over that your body will forget. It doesn't.

You must focus on health after achieving sudden wealth.

6) **Try Not To Burn Out**. Your business was brutal. I know. I've been there. Clients and customers are sometimes hard to deal with. And now you might have employers who just bought your company that you have to report to.

But don't burn out just yet. You need to be responsible and show the people around you that they all made the right decision in trusting you, in buying your business, in buying your goods and services, in working for you, etc. You have few chances in life to demonstrate that you're made of the right stuff and this is one of them.

Keep in Touch

What do you do if you lose it all? Or if you are at a crossroads? If you have some ideas but don't know how to focus them.

Don't worry. Go back to chapter one. Start with the core. I've ridden this roller coaster more times than I would like to admit. Always going back to the core Daily Practice described in chapter One has saved my life every time.

There's no such thing as luck. In the chess-playing world there's a saying: "Only the good players are lucky." That applies to business, health, love, and all forms of success. People can say you were lucky. But the truth is you'll be able to do it again and again, no matter how deeply you fall.

Trust in this and follow these rules and the luck and coincidences that happen on a daily basis will continue forever. Tickling your soul every day.

I hope you like this book. It's my first self-published book. For more on why I self-published, check out jamesaltucher.com.

To ask me questions, follow me on twitter at @jaltucher and ask away. Or email me through jamesaltucher.com

Stay tuned for book 2: "Meetings with Remarkable People"

Made in the USA
Lexington, KY
21 November 2011